THE TIME OF MY FOOTBALL LIFE

(or how I spent my long service leave)

DAVID PICKEN

THE TIME OF MY FOOTBALL LIFE

(or how I spent my long service leave)

DAVID PICKEN

First published in this form in 2019 by Popcorn Press

A division of Fair Play Publishing

PO Box 4101, Balgowlah Heights NSW 2093 Australia

www.popcornpress.com.au

ISBN: 978-1-925914-02-3

E-Book ISBN: 978-1-925914-03-0

© David Picken 2019

The moral rights of the author have been asserted.

All rights reserved. Except as permitted under the Australian Copyright Act 1968 (for example, a fair dealing for the purposes of study, research, criticism or review), no part of this book may be reproduced, stored in a retrieval system, communicated or transmitted in any form or by any means without prior written permission from the Publisher.

Design and typesetting by Retta Laraway, Looksee Design.

All inquiries should be made to the Publisher via sales@fairplaypublishing.com.au

A catalogue record of this book is available from the National Library of Australia.

CONTENTS

INTRODUCTION ix

CHAPTER ONE
Suitcase bust and smells of Sards 1

CHAPTER TWO
Hands on an Australia match ticket 9

CHAPTER THREE
Afghanistan Football Association 22

CHAPTER FOUR
To Hanover for Mexico vs Angola 25

CHAPTER FIVE
Belly Painting 31

CHAPTER SIX
6:52am Train Berlin to Munich 33

CHAPTER SEVEN
Your Women are Great 40

CHAPTER EIGHT
Oh, yes!!! 45

CHAPTER NINE
Testing Germany 57

CONTENTS

CHAPTER TEN
Australia in uncharted waters 59

CHAPTER ELEVEN
Just a bit distorted 65

CHAPTER TWELVE
Played against someone involved in the World Cup!! 71

CHAPTER THIRTEEN
Dortmund: Semi-Final day 76

CHAPTER FOURTEEN
There's buskers and then there's buskers 81

CHAPTER FIFTEEN
Australian product (*sic*) 86

CHAPTER SIXTEEN
The Final 92

APPENDIX
Results and final standings 102

Acknowledgements 113

INTRODUCTION

I played organised, competitive football from the ages of 11 to 45. If I have any ability at all, it is through learning the caper playing "cross gates" with a tennis ball, where the pitch was the cobblestone passage way in the 'backs' of UK Coronation Street style terraced houses and the goals were the opposite rear entrance gates.

I am a lifelong supporter of Port Vale (English League 2 – fourth tier) and, in almost 140 years of history, my club has never been in the Premier League or top tier. Along with Robbie Williams, I was a shareholder in the club through a fan buy out (no longer, though, after the Vale went into administration in 2012 and were bought cheap). Now, after several years of dubioius and inept ownership, Vale has now been returned to the community in the hands of new owners Carol and Kevin Shanahan.

My playing highlights include a couple of seasons in the Staffordshire County Premier League and representing the Western Highlands Province in the 1972 Papua New Guinea national championships. Impressive, eh?!!

I also admit to being a football tragic – when the Vale won promotion to the old Second Division (now called the Championship) in a play off in 1989, I was working in Hong Kong. With no international radio coverage available I called my father in the UK and got him to tape his trannie to the mouthpiece of his 'phone so that I could listen to the second half live via the local radio.

Since 2004, I have been helping out at the Surf Coast Football Club (in Victoria,

INTRODUCTION

Australia) coaching with the senior women's team and various junior sides. Now I help with just minor admin.

In 2006 I had lived in Australia for 11 years and was already bound up in the Australian World Cup myth. I had watched on TV in England in 1974 as an Australian team (part time professionals at best) made the country's first appearance at the tournament in West Germany. Since then, there had been a series of disappointments. As the almost perennial Oceania champions (New Zealand having made the 1982 finals in Spain) and no direct qualifying place, Australia was always faced with a perverse play-off against a country bearing little relevance in terms of location. For example, 1985 they played Scotland (coached by Alex Ferguson) home and away for a place at the Mexico finals - a 2-0 aggregate loss amid rumours of a pitch and game time re-jigged by the authorities to suit the Scots. In 1993, they lost narrowly (2-1 on aggregate) to a Diego Maradona inspired Argentina. There was a dramatic, unbelievable, gut wrenching loss to Iran in 1997 going out on away goals after a draw in Teheran and having led 2-0 in Melbourne in the return. This was among my most disappointing experiences ever watching football. A loss to Uruguay in 2001 followed; the Socceroos having won the first leg in Melbourne. At the time of the play-off qualifier in 2005 against Uruguay again I was an Australian citizen and had begun to feel the pain. For the second leg of the 2005 play-off, I drove to Sydney for the game – somehow convinced that history was to be made. And so it transpired. A heart pumping penalty shoot-out including two saves from Aussie 'keeper Mark Schwarzer, and John Aloisi driving home the deciding kick. Delirious scenes followed as TV and radio commentators lost their composure and fans celebrated into the early hours.

INTRODUCTION

My mind was made up that I had to be at the World Cup in Germany as Australia was about to take the stage for the first time in 32 years. Not to mention England, the country of my birth. This is the story of my journey and experiences.

CHAPTER ONE
SUITCASE BUST AND SMELLS OF SARDS

It could almost be a pastiche song. Try it; it works actually with the music to the first line of 'Me and Bobby McGee.'

My heading comes from the fact that my brand new suitcase arrived in Frankfurt with the shell broken on one corner. Baggage handler error is the only thing I can imagine. It was intact as it slid down the check-in desk belt at Melbourne Airport. The bottle of Sards (an Antipodean miracle fabric cleaner) was for my daughter living in London who had requested a 'Red Cross Parcel' of supplies – you know the sort of thing – tube of Vegemite, dark chocolate Tim Tams, and anything else to keep together the body and soul of an Australian away from home.

Among the requests was one for help in trying to get clothes clean in London's overly hard water. The damn bottle burst at some point between Melbourne and Frankfurt (punctured by the suitcase breakage?), emptied and soaked into a raft of clothing items leaving a pungent aroma of eucalypt. Luckily, I had an early check-in for the Frankfurt hotel giving a bit of time to deal with the miasma. My hotel bedroom resembled a refugee camp – trying to dry the stuff after first submerging it in the hand basin in an attempt to soak out the Sards.

You know why I am in Frankfurt, of course. It's not springtime, but *Weltmeister* time in Germany. The first time I have ever been to a World Cup. After years of planning – eyeing up the fact that my long service leave became due in 2005 – I knew what I wanted to do. Almost 18 months of ticket ballots and very strange first come first served shenanigans (of which more later), have finally come to fruition and I am ready for a good dose of what Roy and HG, two Australian comedians, describe as 'too much football is barely enough.'

The flight over was uneventful until near the end when the captain announced that the family members of Socceroos Josh Kennedy and Josip Skoko were on board and wished their boys and the rest of the squad the best. Josip is a Geelong boy and I could not resist asking where his family were sitting.

I was as pleased as punch to introduce myself to his dad and brother. I asked them to wish Josip all the best from Deakin University in general and the School of Architecture and Building in particular. Josip was a student with us about 11 years ago.

I arrived in Frankfurt at 5:45am on the Friday of the tournament's first game, and very quickly I had one of those, *should I say anything or keep quiet?* experiences. On the train from the airport, I was standing next to a group of Aussies trying to make some sense of the rail system map. "*Where did we get on?*" and "*Where do we get off?*" kind of thing.

When I offered, "*It's the next stop.*" They wondered how I could tell. Well, it was a veritable mass of coloured lines for sure. However, a fairly large aeroplane symbol meant you didn't need to understand the word *Flughafen*, and the station with the largest label by far with Frankfurt am Main doesn't actually translate to Frankfurt main station (Frankfurt sits on the Main river), and so you didn't need to understand the word *Hauptbahnof* either, the label was so large.

Anyway, they went on to ponder the wisdom of booking seats on future journeys to Australia's matches. I suggested that they go to the *Deutsche Bahn* (DB) website for the German railway system which is excellent and gives the info on whether you would be advised to reserve a seat, and when it is compulsory to

(OR HOW I SPENT MY LONG SERVICE LEAVE)

reserve a seat. In acknowledging this, they said they had a monthly rail pass which allows them ten travel days within the period of their one month stay.

Their month, I thought, having arrived on 9th June, and if they trigger the validity on 10th June, will just squeak them through to Final Day on 9th July. However, they had better make sure they have that tenth travel day still available on 9th July and that there is a train from Berlin to Frankfurt after the final ends around 10:30pm. Being stuck in Berlin would be no hardship – it's a great city, but it does not have direct flights to Melbourne.

And this is where my, *'should I say anything or keep quiet?'* moment arose. I intended to crisscross Germany in the coming five weeks, attending my FIFA imposed maximum of seven matches (one person can only obtain tickets for seven matches through the official ticket shop) – and only one of mine is an Australia game, and that ticket was obtained just ten days before my departure date.

I will elaborate later on why that ticket came so late, but patience please. I would be crisscrossing Germany going to games and watching on the big screen at Fan Fests in the game city for other Socceroos games. By sheer luck I found out from the DB website several months before that, for the duration of the tournament, there was a *Weltmeister* pass – go anywhere, anytime, travel every day, and several times a day if you like.

It cost 349 Euro for 34 days of unlimited travel. No need to worry about a ten day constraint. Very thoughtfully, I felt, the validity was set to run from two days before the tournament started until two days after the tournament ended. The normal tourist 'ten days only of travel within a calendar month' pass which my travelling companions had was clearly a much more restrictive affair and cost 280 Euro. With a one way trip from Berlin to Frankfurt at around 100 Euro, as the saying goes, '*You do the math.*' So should I have said something or not? I didn't. What was the point? What can be done? Almost certainly nothing. So why upset them?

On the Friday morning and during the day leading up to the tournament's opening match (Germany as hosts would play Ecuador in Munich), I wandered around the beautiful city of Frankfurt. I found a square in the Römer district – very picturesque with lovely old, timbered buildings. Many cities and towns in west European countries have squares like this – they are a delight. Already, at an early hour, this square had signs of being taken over by the England fans. They were there a day ahead of time for the match against Paraguay on the Saturday.

Small groups of fans sat at tables chatting. Some were drinking coffee, others were already into the amber fluid. I mean to say, be reasonable, it was 7:30am and the sun was up over the yard arm! There was an old London double decker bus in the colours of a UK Building Society, a major sponsor of the England team. Fans were invited to scrawl messages to their heroes. "*Bring the World Cup over to mine, Becks!!! xx Susan*" or some such. It was plastered with them. St George's Cross flags were draped from walls. It was, though, fairly quiet.

I was on my way to check out the Frankfurt Fan Fest site. In each of the World Cup venue cities, the organisers had set up a temporary public arena with huge TV screens where those without tickets could watch the game – and sample, somewhat vicariously perhaps, the atmosphere.

In Frankfurt, very imaginatively, they set up two massive screens down the centre of the River Main, one screen facing each bank, and temporary grandstands from which to view. So despite what people might tell you about the stringent security checks on ticket holders – personalised tickets containing microchips

(OR HOW I SPENT MY LONG SERVICE LEAVE)

with the registered holder's passport details we were told – these checks were not about hooliganism (although a former miscreant registered by the authorities would not have received a ticket in the first place). They were to avoid ticket scalping.

In the past, a World Cup organising committee would have been saying, "*If you don't have tickets, don't come to Germany.*" The Fan Fest sites were the antithesis of this – entry was free and there was no ID check. Presumably, the authorities had border checks in place in an effort to corral the would-be troublemakers who had a history.

On my way back to the Fan Fest site later to watch the opening match of the tournament, I walked via the square in Römer and things were much livelier. In fact, it was heaving with England supporters. Now it was a little more (a lot more actually)... how shall I say... rabid. England chants were all around. There were more St George's Cross flags.

The England flag is a very convenient flag for adding slogans. It has become very much the thing to do – a flag with a slogan – to get the name of your club or your locale on the telly. I've got a banner with, "*Surf Coast F.C. Torquay, Australia*" in club colours – blue letters on a yellow background if you were looking for it. There was humour with Walmington-on-Sea (of Dad's Army fame) across the horizontal red stripe of one England flag! Each white square of the St George's Cross flag can be filled with a letter and so you see, for example, BWFC, and the horizontal red stripe enlightens you with, "*Bolton 'til I die.*"

There were the God botherers at such gatherings, of course, folks with placards saying, "John 10.12" "*The End is Nigh*" or something similar. Then there is the humour at their expense with a guy wearing a tee shirt with the message, "*Jesus Saves... but Rooney nets the rebound!!*"

England supporters' really are amongst the best at this caper.

All of the banter was good natured. The official slogan of this World Cup was "A *time to make friends*" and everyone in service positions seemed to be making an effort, though not in any forced way. German railways, *Deutsche Bahn*, was the leader.

From time to time a group of German fans would snake through the square on their way to the Fan Fest and were greeted with the chant, "*Who are ya, who are ya, who are ya?*" It was delivered in a somewhat menacing tone, it's true, but the Germans took it with aplomb and almost a bow, as if to say, "*Good to see you here. Let's hope it's a feast of football.*"

One England fan emerged from the throng carrying, with his hand cupped under the fuselage, a 1.5 metre long inflatable model of a Spitfire in battle paintwork. He swooped alongside the line of Germans as if to buzz them. For a second it seemed like a, "*Don't mention the war*" moment, but it was just a butterfly-like movement, not sustained or threatening, for he was in and out in a second or two. Meant in jest and taken that way.

Did I say this mob was rabid? Well, as you approached the square, six or seven footballs were flying through the air, this way and that. As you got closer you could hear the thump of the kickers' boots as they launched the balls on an upward arc. It was if they were being fired from several cannons at random.

At first it seemed potentially dangerous, but the square was so large, and every ball was being lobbed from the edge towards the centre and back, never reaching the surrounding buildings at any pace and most often being intercepted by a would-be kicker. The mob was large, random, a heaving mass, and it suddenly struck me that football in historical times was like this – which is still re-enacted

(OR HOW I SPENT MY LONG SERVICE LEAVE)

in England every Shrove Tuesday actually - reportedly with origins in the 1100s; *Calcio Storico* in Florence, likewise, a game originating in the 1500s (although it can be disturbingly violent).

In the English version unlimited numbers on each side, goals miles apart, a rabid mob engaged in a tussle. Every so often the ball appears and, probably in just the same manner, is heaved aloft in a parabolic arc only to disappear again within the crowd. In fact, the exchange in the Frankfurt square more resembled kick to kick practice in Australian Rules Football.

The next day, when I took some recently arrived friends to Römer before we went over to the stadium for the England vs Paraguay game, the balls were flying again - just as safely I have to add, but clearly the authorities had been advised of the previous day's fun. The local constabulary were doing very passable impersonations of those killjoys you see in the stadium at some events - the happy thought police beach ball snafflers. England vs Paraguay was my very first game at a World Cup finals tournament. The game itself was not overly memorable. England largely controlled the game and had several scoring chances although the final result - a win to England - was courtesy of an own goal.

For me the excitement of just being there was enough. The England starting XI contained some big names - David Beckham, Michael Owen, Steven Gerrard and Frank Lampard, for example - at the time, very much at the height of their powers. I finally believed that my diligent efforts in obtaining tickets, starting some two years before, were worthwhile.

For this game my ticket had come through orthodox means and really quite easily. I had been advised by a friend in early 2005 that the only way to obtain tickets for England games was to become a member of the official England supporters association. Each participating country would receive an allocation of tickets and with England, at least, my friend told me, there would be a fair allocation process for association members.

The allocation would be by ballot with a weighting based on the number of games a member had attended within a designated period in preceding years. A sort of loyalty system if you will. In addition, the level of membership which entitled you to an entry in the ballot was capped. My good fortune was that my friend's advice came in time for me to gain membership right on the cusp of the cap being reached.

I might mention that there is a small elite of England supporters, my friend included, who follow England home and away without fail. They were certain of a ticket for every England game in Germany. I remember thinking at the time that Australia does not have an official supporters association so how is that going to work? Not to mention employing a similar loyalty system could be somewhat onerous – for example, attending even a home game in Sydney is quite an ask for someone living in Perth.

Group B – Opening match

10 June 2006, FIFA WM Stadion Frankfurt, Frankfurt

England   1 : 0   Paraguay

Carlos Gamarra 3' (OG)

Referee: Marco Rodríguez (Mexico)

Attendance: 48,000

CHAPTER TWO
HANDS ON AN AUSTRALIA MATCH TICKET

I picked up my ticket for the Australia vs Croatia game on the Friday morning at 6:00am at the Sheraton Convention Centre near Frankfurt Airport. No worry about travelling out there by train and back – my *Weltmeister* Pass covered it.

The Sheraton was where FFA Travel had set up camp for a couple days before the Kaiserslautern game against Japan. Football Federation Australia Travel – remember that name, FFA **Travel** (emphasis added), it is important later. I am not completely sure whether FFA Travel existed before the World Cup qualification. Maybe it did, but certainly not in its then current incarnation.

For FFA Travel you can read Fanatics if you like. You know, those folks who developed their reputation as Davis Cup cheerleaders – and, fair play, they, along with Newc, Roachie and the lads did a great job in Nice those few years ago. However, what, in 2005/06, did the Fanatics know about football? What did they know about selling World Cup finals tickets? I did not know the answer to that, but I did know that after the drama of the November shoot out against Uruguay, FFA apparently handed over the right to deal with its World Cup ticket allocation to the Fanatics.

The Fanatics' leader, Warren Livingstone, after the debacle of the first come-first served email system they devised, is on record as saying that the Fanatics were the only organisation in Australia, at that point in time, capable of organising such an exercise. Tickemaster and Ticketek would question Wozzer's assertion, me thinks.

At 6:00am there wasn't much traffic, so I spent a minute or two with one of the FFA (Travel) staff. Turned out, she was really a full-time FFA employee and wearing a FFA Travel polo shirt. All this is relevant when I come to my theory about ticket allocation – namely, if I could put it this way, FFA Travel was masquerading as 'the' FFA. I had a grumble or two with the woman about the way the FFA had allocated its share of the tickets.

"Why didn't you use a ballot system? Why wasn't it web based? Why did you require people to give their credit card details in an open email?"

Yes, that's right they spurned protection through encryption, which is pretty well mandatory for any organisation involved in selling via the internet. And you did have to put your credit card details in an open email.

However, then it got really interesting, when the lady offered, "Well, FIFA would not allow us to do the allocation via the web."

"Pardon?"

"No, no... honestly, I was in the meetings with the FIFA Head of Ticketing."

So, picture this. There is this guy from Switzerland, Head of Ticketing from one of, if not the wealthiest sporting organisations in the world, FIFA telling FFA that they could not allocate the tickets via the web. That they could not use a system, which is probably as close as you can get to fairness in the electronic world. This compared with the inequity, as any IT professional will tell you, of everyone clicking 'send' on an email message at 9:00am + one nanosecond precisely on the same date.

(OR HOW I SPENT MY LONG SERVICE LEAVE)

So why did FIFA use a web-based system for its own ticketing system – the official central Ticket Shop – which used a phased sequence of ballots and first come, first served processes? I knew they had because that is how I obtained tickets. Why did the England FA distribute its allocation via a web site - and through a ballot as it happens? I know this because I obtained tickets through their system too.

Why would FIFA require FFA to use a system which exposed every Australian applicant to the credit card fraud, which has the international banking system frightened out of its collective skin? It doesn't make sense, does it? Well, I wouldn't have thought so. My theory is that FFA allowed itself, for the purpose of the ticket distribution exercise, to become FFA Travel.

You see, if you were an applicant you would have seen on the web-based promo that what they were about was selling holiday packages with World Cup tickets. TFrom the top, as it were, there was Package A – super deluxe accommodation, tour guides including former players Robbie Slater and Frank Farina (former coach too), this, that and the other perk, go to Socceroos training sessions etc, etc. You had to go way down the list to find the package where you applied for tickets only.

My theory is that the FIFA Head of Ticketing would not allow FFA to sell tickets via the web in the name of FIFA, if FFA was about selling holiday packages that included tickets. Remember you had to scroll down through all the other options before you got to the 'tickets only' section. What is certain is that the England FA's approach was about selling tickets only. If you wanted advice on travel and accommodation, there was a link on their web site to a separate company for holidays only.

I suspect that was the FIFA-approved method of selling tickets. One more thing to note is that the England Fans organisation had just three people in Germany for the whole tournament – because they were only dealing with tickets.

At the Sheraton Hotel, FFA (Travel) had seven staff on duty and more were arriving as I left, plus half a dozen locally hired security guards.

Were applications for super deluxe packages given some sort of preference? We certainly were not told that in the application information. I mean, if it really was first come, first served, there could have been a few thousand fastest first fingers, so to speak, just looking for tickets - and Robbie and Frank would have been out of a job!

Odd isn't it that in the imbroglio that followed the 20th December date that FFA Travel produced statistics to show there was a nice, pretty well 50/50 split between successful travel plus tickets applicants against those who only wanted tickets? It is of course, entirely possible those statistics were correct.

That's the thing with some elements of statistics, it's about chance and probability. However, I cannot help but think of George Negus interviewing a Suharto family member before an Indonesian election. "So, what sort of majority do you think you will get?" asked George. "Oh, I think we will get around 94.6% of the vote," she replied with not a glimmer of feeling. George, for once, was speechless and you would be, wouldn't you?

Getting to the game

I mentioned that *Deutsche Bahn* was in the lead in the service stakes. At that stage DB were winning the "Fantastic Service award" from me. Their web site is brilliant – you can search it to find train times having entered start and finish locations and, either, when you would like to leave or when you would like to

(OR HOW I SPENT MY LONG SERVICE LEAVE)

arrive. For the World Cup, it was often a case of when do you need to arrive, and that question is important, so it is clever to include that option.

The ordering and delivery of my *Weltmeister* pass (WMP) was dealt with very efficiently. Before leaving Australia, I decided that it would pay my daughter to obtain one even though she was only coming over from London for four days (the Croatia game and a bit of travelling around). Shortly before I left Australia I sent an email to *Herr* Ulrich Meister, who had been so helpful when I purchased my pass. I added a message saying it needed to be with her quickly.

The next day my mobile rang. It was one of *Herr* Meister's colleagues checking when the pass must reach my daughter and assuring me it would be in the post that very day. They even left a message on my home phone to confirm it had, indeed, been posted. One more thing – I booked my Frankfurt hotel online via the DB web site. They certainly got the prize for their unmatched service in my experience.

On the train from Berlin to Kaiserslautern (via Mannheim), DB, to use an apt metaphor, banged another goal in. I heard the ticket collector's tones down the carriage – so went for the WMP – but as he got to my seat I saw he wasn't checking tickets at all, "*Guten Morgen… bitteschön*" – he's offering us all little chokkies and not checking tickets!

There were lots of Aussies on this particular train from Berlin and my carriage was dotted with yellow; my supporter's scarf was draped across the top of one the windows, an Australian flag over another. Plenty of people admiried my 1974 inspired commemorative jersey.

"Hey mate, that's a bloody ripper." In particular, they admired the lovely embroidered badge. That was interesting because, being the card carrying pedant that I am, I wondered why our 2006 jersey was one of only a couple out of 32 countries that has a printed badge – an embroidered one looks so much more classy!

As we travelled to Kaiserslautern everyone was happy. It was a sort of serene happiness born of how good it felt for Australia to be back on the World Cup stage. I pondered for a moment. "Let's hope we are still happy at the end of the day."

Well, now we know how happy. What a day for Australian football! I was at the match! I was going to several World Cup matches over the next four weeks. I had been planning this for a few years. Over the previous 18 months I had been through the wringer applying for tickets through any ballot or other process I could find. There are references to this elsewhere, but for now let's just say that my only 'legal' ticket for Australia was the Croatia game – Australia's last game at the group stages of the tournament.

As I mentioned earlier, notice of securing that ticket came very late – ten days before I was due to leave for Germany. My fellow applicants and I had been unsuccessful first time round. I assume some people had not taken up their offers and FFA Travel were offering them to those of us who missed out. While I had a ticket for just one match, my plan had always been to go to each city for our games for the atmosphere.

The World cup organisers set up official big screen sites, called Fan Fest sites: think Federation Square in Melbourne or London's Hyde Park where many major events are screened live on massive screens for those that do not have tickets for the event venue. The World Cup organisers knew thousands would travel to Germany without tickets just to be there and it was a very clever idea.

(OR HOW I SPENT MY LONG SERVICE LEAVE)

So, off to the Fan Fest via the 6:06am train from Berlin to Kaiserslautern for Australia's first game against Japan. The train from Mannheim was jammed with Aussies and Japanese – a mass of yellow shirts and blue shirts. By pure chance, at the station change, I continued a conversation with a bloke and his son from Murwillumbah in northern New South Wales.

Some years ago, the major player among United Kingdom ticket scalpers was a man who rejoiced in the entirely appropriate moniker of 'Stan Flashman' (I do believe it was his real name). Well, Son of Stan was on the train – in the carriage I had chosen – "Psssst, wanna buy a ticket?" Although, as I recall Stan was never that subtle. I paid 100 Euro for a 60 Euro ticket – good mark up for him but not that bad for me.

Now, this next bit is tricky material. The ticket was printed with … wait for it … 'Football Federation Australia' and then a number not a name. So, we cannot tell which FFA connected person was the first purchaser of this ticket. From whose personal allocation has this ticket come? This bloke had a wad of tickets in his bag – I saw them – all on a continuous strip as they had come off the printer. Clearly not a shonky printer I should add – from the hologram and compared with others they certainly looked kosher. Not only that, his mate next to him had a pile of tickets, and another bloke behind me had more! They were working together. Where the bloody hell had they got them from? Before me, a Japanese girl had bought a couple from 'Stan.' Actually his business card (honest, he had a business card) said 'Jack,' with a telephone number, I kid you not!).

Not sure how the Japanese girl was proposing to get past any security check with a FFA endorsed ticket. Answer – there was no check at the turnstile. Such a mass of people queuing and careful bag checking (even taking your plastic water bottle away) they had precious little time for checking the ticket holder's credentials.

There were people around me on the train who, while perfectly happy that I had got a ticket, were rolling their eyes and saying, "What the...?" Probably thinking about a mate back home who didn't get a ticket through the terrible FFA first come, first served fiasco – because FFA officials and cronies were gifting themselves tickets they always intended to pass on to the Stan Flashman types.

All of this aside, I was thrilled to be at that first game and even more so between the 82nd and 90th minute! Australia, 1-0 down, came back dramatically. Tim Cahill notched Australia's first ever World Cup finals goals, and then another before John Aloisi wrapped it up. There was a lot of hugging and kissing people you had never met before as in Australia's dramatic qualifying match against Uruguay last year. Among all this, though, I did fret that in buying the ticket in this manner I am fuelling this scalping.

Another thing you will not believe is that I chose this particular packed carriage (not the one in front or behind) and I probably would not have seen the scalper if I hadn't been tapped on the shoulder by Phil, a mate from the UK who I know through our support of Port Vale (our hometown team in Stoke-on-Trent in England – same one as Robbie Williams). He bought two tickets just after the Japanese girl and had spotted me as he weaved his way down the carriage. "Eh up, Dave, fancy meeting you ... erm ... this bloke is selling tickets, you know."

The tickets were consecutively numbered – I sat next to Phil and his mate at the match! A couple of weeks before, when I was wondering about the possibilities of yet another ballot I had gone in for, my friend Jim Smith said, "It will happen, Dave, the planets are aligned." I thought about that too – so maybe the ticket on

(OR HOW I SPENT MY LONG SERVICE LEAVE)

the train was meant to be. It must have been – I ended up hanging my Surf Coast FC banner in the only spot really available – right at the back of the stand opposite the players' entrance tunnel – next to a St George Cross with Port Vale FC on it! Don't know where the PVFC guys were sitting – but I do know it belonged to some Stoke lads we had bumped in to in Frankfurt on the previous Saturday.

I don't think I have been much prouder than when we sang the anthem before the game. I hope it came over well on telly, but it was a spine-tingler for sure. The boys would have to have been pumped. In the finish, it was just great to see them plug away and not give up. We, in the crowd, sort of stopped singing for a bit there in the middle of the second half.

Maybe thinking that it looks like one of those days. What about Hiddink's substitutions? Takes off a defender and brings on an attacker. Entirely logical of course, if you are losing, but how many have the courage to do it? It was a comeback Liverpool and Manchester United would have been proud of. What price now the autograph I got from Tim Cahill in Hong Kong airport a few weeks beforehand – me returning from a work trip to Italy and Tim returning for World Cup preparations?

After the game my friends and I went back to Frankfurt and had a couple of drinks at their hotel before I caught the 01:01 overnighter back to Berlin. As we watched the Italy vs Ghana game in the hotel lounge, I was explaining how there would be a Fan Fest type of set-up back in Melbourne at Federation Square. Then, right on cue, during the half-time break German TV news showed the assembled multitudes at Fed Square going bonkers at Tim Cahill's equaliser and then going whatever is more than bonkers as first Cahill and then John Aloisi notched two more.

THE TIME OF MY FOOTBALL LIFE

I had a fitful night's sleep on the train back to Berlin. I had just settled in to the reserved seat when the carriage filled with a tour group from Argentina. Despite it being past 1 o'clock in the morning they talked on and on, loudly. Even ear plugs and noise cancelling headphones were no use.

Group F – Opening match

12 June 2006, Fritz Walter Stadium, Kaiserslautern

Australia   3 : 1   Japan

Cahill 84', 89'   Nakamura 26'

Aloisi 90+2'

Referee: Essam Abd El Fatah (Egypt)

Attendance: 46,000

Bleary eyed, I arrived in Berlin at 6:46am – my WM Pass took me back to Lichterfelde West in the Berlin suburbs – removed the bike from the lock up and rode home. I slept for a few hours and then, later in the day, I was off to the Brandenburg Gate Fan Fest to see if Brazil could do Australia a favour and beat Croatia.

According to TV reports there were 50,000 people at the Berlin Fan Fest to watch Brazil's first game of the tournament on the big screen. The game itself was also the first of the tournament to be held at Berlin's refurbished Olympic Stadium – the one where Jesse Owens caused Hitler embarrassment in 1936.

On my way to the Fan Fest I stopped by the famous department store KaDeWe

(OR HOW I SPENT MY LONG SERVICE LEAVE)

in Wittenberg Platz. They are famous for stocking anything and everything. You can actually buy Vegemite and Tim Tams there! I was after the Australian away jersey – I've already got plenty of yellow and I thought we might be in the away colours against Brazil.

In fact, the Australian stock in the Nike shop of this world famous store is minimal. Australia's away jersey? You must be joking! There were just five Socceroos jerseys against racks full of many other countries including their home and away kit. Trinidad and Tobago, Togo, Ivory Coast, and Ghana were lowish too. Perhaps they have sold out of ours! I jested with the shop assistant suggesting to him they were not taking us seriously.

I always wanted to go to Brazil and watch football, play football, learn how they coach football. The first time I ever got the chance to choose what kit a team would play in, I chose yellow shirts with green trim, blue shorts, and white socks. Maybe if I dressed the team in the right colours by some strange osmosis, we would play samba style football too. Tragic, isn't it?

That night I got the chance to be in the midst of Brazilians watching football. It was an education. Samba bands, flags flying, a sea of yellow and green. Beautiful women cruising by. The supporters feel every move, every kick, every nuance of their team's play. Even the slightest touch or flick that looks like the player has the ball on a string is greeted with a murmur of ecstasy. If the trick comes off and fools the opposing player, leaving them lunging at thin air or prostrate in the Brazilian player's wake, it brings a raucous cheer and a chorus of whistles.

It must be wonderful to be a Brazilian player when your supporters are so knowledgeable, possibly even not too shabby themselves in the football juggling department (and that's only the women), because they see all these moves and tricks, however small and subtle, and cheer them enthusiastically. Like any performer responding to audience reaction, you would do your tricks again and again, and hone them and develop new ones. You would, wouldn't you, if the audience reaction drug gets to you?

The favourite trick, at least in terms of crowd reaction was 'the nutmeg' – the English term for when a player in possession of the ball feints one way then the other in an effort to deceive and, if the opportunity arises, passes it between his opponent's legs.

The wrong footed opponent looks like a goose and the Brazilian crowd loves it. Then it was done to the Brazilian captain … erm … ooh, that's not in the plan. Not happy, I would say was the response from the Brazilian supporters when, pardon the pun, the boot was on the other foot.

In the end it was, perhaps, a partly stuttering performance from Brazil. A gem of a goal from Kaká for a 1-0 win. Croatia had chances and looked as if they would be strong opposition in what might prove to be a pivotal, last group match for Australia. Important for us, though, that Brazil beat them – a more comprehensive win would have suited us better. However, let's look no further for fear of tempting fate.

It really was a classic case of one game at a time. Let's have a big effort against Brazil. Stop them scoring if we can and let our more creative players, Kewell, Bresciano, Viduka, and Emerton do what they will – keep the Brazilians too busy defending themselves. The hard work on the track that Guus Hiddink had been putting our lads through, and which we had heard so much about, would stand them in good stead.

As I left the Fan Fest there were several two-person roaming TV crews looking

(OR HOW I SPENT MY LONG SERVICE LEAVE)

for a sound bite. I think being a pretty girl seemed to be the key requirement for the crew to home in on. One was interviewing a Brazilian girl and as they pulled away looking for their next victim I asked if they were from Brazilian television. "No, we are from the BBC." Feeling cheeky, I suggested that the quote for Brazilian Television would be, "Australia – top of the group!!!" I did not get invited to broadcast to the world, but rather got a sniff and a disdainful look that indicated it wasn't news.

Fair warning – they were not taking us seriously enough, I fancied.

CHAPTER THREE
AFGHANISTAN FOOTBALL ASSOCIATION

In the first episode of this diary, I took a swipe at the distribution approach adopted by Football Federation Australia with its allocation of match tickets for the games involving Australia. In addition, I pondered on the question of how ticket scalpers on the train to Kaiserslautern had shoulder bags full of tickets endorsed with 'Football Federation Australia.'

I can now say the plot had begun to thicken. The friends from the UK that I mentioned meeting had made a trip to Leipzig between our meeting in Frankfurt for England's first game and then later on the train to Kaiserslautern. They went to Leipzig ticketless on the day of the Serbia and Montenegro vs Netherlands game, fully anticipating being able to obtain tickets from some source or other.

I might add this World Cup tournament was the sixth they have attended so they had seen it all before. They did, indeed, procure tickets in Leipzig, and which national association, was the source of these scalped tickets? Unbelievably, they were endorsed with the words 'Afghanistan Football Association'!! I saw the tickets.

Now, we could speculate for hours on the pathway of these tickets to Germany and would be none the wiser. Why on earth would officials of the Afghanistan Football Association seek tickets for Serbia and Montenegro vs Netherlands? I did not even try to guess.

(OR HOW I SPENT MY LONG SERVICE LEAVE)

Before I left Australia, I had heard an interview on the ABC's PM programme between Mark Colvin and Andrew Jennings, the British author, whose book, *Lords of the Rings*, examines the backroom dealings of the International Olympic Committee. Jennings had then turned his attention to FIFA.

On the PM programme, he made the claim that for anyone in Germany who is offered a ticket by an unofficial seller, then the source of that ticket is from the "back door of FIFA," by way of international association officials, 'the sports blazers' Jennings called them, who sell their allocation of tickets to make a bit on the side.

The brighter side of life

There was a fantastic atmosphere in Germany, and it seemed to gather momentum with each day of the tournament. I'm not sure if this increasing energy was dependent on Germany's continued presence into the later stages, but it was a really exciting place to be at that time.

Friends who have no particular love for football were caught up in it all and were just loving the *joie de vivre* (or should I say *lebenslust*). There were literally thousands of people there from across the world; among many, I would identify the Scots who, let's face it are premier league when it comes to partying, were there and they didn't even qualify for the final stages. Who cares? It was a football feast and a fun feast.

If Germany was still in business on 9th July for the Final, the country would go pop for sure.

The German team did much to stoke the boiler a couple nights before; waiting until the 91st minute, into additional time allowed by the referee for earlier stoppages, before snatching a 1-0 win against Poland. Oliver Neuville slid in a goal from David Odonkor's cross to the delight of the Germans in the crowd and millions watching on television. Both players were late substitutions made by coach Jurgen Klinsmann. For Poland, it was an all or nothing game having lost their opening game to Ecuador 2-0. The Poles provided stern opposition and could easily have taken the game. As it was, they were on the way home.

An underlying, yet important aspect of this clash was that it seemed, with the exception of a small number of preventive arrests, to have passed off without any crowd problems. According to television reports Poland had, in recent times, begun to suffer from the worst kind of football supporter violence and hooliganism at its national league matches.

From the moment the two countries were drawn in the same group in last December's draw, the propensity of some Polish supporters for violence and the proximity of the two countries had been exercising the minds of authorities. Mercifully, that Wednesday night passed off largely without incident.

And so we partied on.

CHAPTER FOUR
TO HANOVER FOR MEXICO vs ANGOLA

On Thursday 15th June I made the short (1 hour 40 minutes) trip to Hanover for Mexico vs Angola in Group C on the DB Intercity Express (ICE). The modern ICEs have a digital notice board in each carriage showing the destination and intermediate stops. From time to time the train speed was displayed. The top speed I saw on my trips was 247kph (almost 150mph in the old money). Now that is a high speed train – not a bullet train, it's true, but certainly deserving of the high speed tag.

On arrival at Hanover *Hauptbahnof* (main station), it was clear that the place was *Casa Mexicana!!* It was absolutely jumping. The station's main concourse and its square were thronged with Mexican supporters – chanting, sounding horns and whistles.

The word cacophony really doesn't do the noise justice. Many sombreros in evidence for a Pancho Villa look, and some had delved deeper into Mexican history for Aztec influenced costumes and headdresses of peacock tail feathers.

Unending group photos – "The team" in Hanover, as it were, seemed to be the theme. There was a smaller number of Angolan supporters but equally vibrant with their red, yellow, and black colours. Supporters of both sides were mixing easily in a riot of colour with the green, red, and white of the Mexicans.

The streets radiating out from the station towards the stadium and the Fan

Fest were all jammed with people. Restaurants and bars were doing a roaring trade. Kick off was at 9:00pm, the last game of the day across the country, so everyone was having dinner and a pre-game drink.

We notice a guy, Mexican supporter, preparing a contraption that is of the bicycle species – I say species because it was made up of bike components, but this thing was like no bike I had ever seen. The whole thing was leaning against a street lamp and he was standing on a ladder organising things, threading chains, and so on. There were two seats, so it was like a tandem, but that issimplifying things somewhat. It was sort of like three bike frames stacked on top of one another with extra bits of connecting tubing.

It looked as if the riders would sit on the top most bike frame, with extra cogs and chains to transfer the drive down to the wheels. A few minutes later he has got the thing moving – riding as a singleton, no-one willing to take that other seat no doubt - he must have been three metres above the ground. He was last seen disappearing down *Georgstrasse* and no accidents I can report.

World Cup 2006 had various Official Partners, main sponsors to you and me. You would have seen their logos displayed on the green boards positioned behind after-match interviewees. Elsewhere they were in evidence in a variety of ways, some more prominent than others.

Continental, the tyre company, was one of these partners, and in Hanover their promotion in the main station square called for a circular cage, perhaps five metres across with mini football goals diametrically opposed. The punters lined up in pairs to have a go for a three minute session of one on one. I watched for a short while and several pairs came forward to try out their various tricks in an effort to score. Then, two fairly portly, not exactly athletic, customers stepped

(OR HOW I SPENT MY LONG SERVICE LEAVE)

forward. One, to my eye South American looking, clearly knew what he was doing and he was two up pretty smartly. The announcer called out, "*Eine minute,*" (one minute to go), so the South American obviously thought it was time for his party piece.

Some years ago the Columbians had a goalie named René Higuita. René was nicknamed '*El Loco*' for reasons which will become obvious. Modern coaches bang on about decision-making being critical for players. René certainly made odd decisions. For example, he would come way out of goal and join in the outfield play. On one occasion, at least, he was made to look like an idiot during a World Cup game in 1990 against Cameroon when, going to beat one man too many on the dribble, he was robbed of the ball and the opposition's Roger Milla rolled it into an open goal.

René produced perhaps his most spectacular moment at the old Wembley Stadium. The stadium was a shrine to many worldwide and perhaps René, playing his one and only game there, thought, 'This is the time to unfurl my best.' An England player lobbed a shot towards the goal, not particularly hard and coming in about waist high. René could have gathered it easily on the full. Never one to make something easy if there was chance of making it difficult, he dived forward, allowed the ball to pass over him, flicked up both his legs and beat out the ball with a mule kick!! Extraordinary!

I don't recall what the commentator said but I do believe he almost choked.

Well, our portly friend in the *Continental* cage was obviously a devotee of the Higuita philosophy, and he repeated the same trick having first juggled the ball up onto his knee for a couple touches and then up in the air for the scorpion kick – he didn't score but the crowd loved it.

THE TIME OF MY FOOTBALL LIFE

In Hanover, the Fan Fest was smaller than most but no less vibrant and was quite near the stadium. As you neared both locations, there was a sort of doubling of the traffic. The whole area was throbbing to the sound of music, the locals seemed to have pitched it the Latin way, with the Mexican supporters clearly the largest in number. It sounded like a fiesta and anything with a Latino beat was the thing for the bands. It wasn't long before the distinctive sound of the intro to *La Bamba* was heard and the crowd noise went up a cog or two. Overdrive actually, as we were already in top gear.

As the tournament moved on, various aspects of the services improved. This was to be the third game I attended and things such as security checks and the catering provisions, improved each time. It was clear that a lot of thinking had gone into the most minute aspects of the event.

You could take issue with some, for example, plastic bottles of water to keep you hydrated in the warm summer weather (check out the drinks bottles for the players along the touch line for each game), but they were not allowed to be taken into the stadium by spectators. I suppose you could have thrown a plastic bottle full of water, but then again, if it's a question of something with a bit of weight behind it, you could throw your camera or your shoe!

Despite the protestations to the contrary, obviously the prohibition was sought by those with the stadium catering contract. Their intent being to maximise their sales, rather than have folks bringing in bottles filled with your own tap water. When you purchased their water, by the way, it was served in a plastic cup for which you paid a 1 Euro deposit. It was not flimsy plastic but was substantial and reusable. The deposit was to encourage people to return the cups and not leave them strewn on the ground. It had a World Cup logo and I kept one of mine

(OR HOW I SPENT MY LONG SERVICE LEAVE)

– foregoing the deposit for a cheap bit of memorabilia.

On this matter of objects liable to be used as missiles, friends tell me that at other such events in Europe they have had the experience of having tubes of sunscreen confiscated. I wondered whether the organisers could be leaving themselves open to some sort of legal action from people who suffer from heat stroke by forcing customers to buy water which could quite easily be brought with them from home at no cost?

Before the game we went to find a place for dinner. The early evening game in this group was being shown on several plasma screens dotted around the restaurant – it was the Netherlands vs Ivory Coast (ooops, sorry, I mean Côte d'Ivoire – I had read in my team guide that there is a law in Côte d'Ivoire which seeks to enshrine the French and ban the use of the English translation).

Maybe German is okay as the papers didn't seem to bother – they use *Elfenbeinkuste*. The restaurant was packed but the efficiency and speed with which they knocked out the meals were amazing. This was the second game to have taken place in Hanover and what they had learned from the first one had been put to good use. I say this because I had noticed improvement of service delivery in other areas too. Whenever I returned to a facility or used a World Cup related service, a little grumble I had initially, had been addressed.

The first time I entered one of the Fan Fest areas they would not allow anyone to take in even empty plastic water bottles. The system of barriers to control the hordes was non-existent (hard to believe this was not thought of before but it was certainly corrected) and my impression was that they had drafted in more security staff. The 'no plastic water bottles' was an odd one, when you consider it had been really hot and there was the danger of dehydration. They did sell water along with other beverages at the accredited kiosks inside, and that left you wondering what the real reason for the plastic bottle ban was. Two days after Frankfurt, I went to the Berlin fan fest and the plastic bottles were now okay.

The security clearance at each match was an area that improved but became no less strict. In Hanover, there was a capacity crowd of 46,000 and yet every bag was searched, and everyone was frisked.

The first step was a preliminary ticket check. Do you even have a ticket for this game? Should you even be in this security check in the first place? I noticed that all staff were well mannered – an all clear concluded with a smile and an unhurried, "*Enjoy the game,*" that was not from the fast food restaurant training manual (that produces the wooden 'have a nice day' style). I was convinced these people were serious. The frisk and bag search are not superficial and is done with a smile.

We were inside the stadium. One of twelve for the tournament, either brand new or entirely refurbished for the tournament. The three I had now visited were all impressive. Steeply sloping seating giving excellent views to just about all spectators. Some seats were designated as 'obstructed view.'

Typically, this can mean you were seated in the front row of a section or tier, and even though it was only a rail in front, because of the steep slope you may have a slight obstruction only when the play is immediately beneath you. A tip – as a rule, if all you can get is obstructed view seats then take them.

CHAPTER FIVE
BELLY PAINTING

And so to the Mexico vs Angola game – but not before I tell you about belly painting. As you might guess, the face painters were working overtime in Germany and some creations extended the 'face' element more than somewhat. Hair was coloured, as were upper arms, while sometimes the face painting was just a delicate tri-colour on each cheek.

Our seat allocation placed us within the Mexican supporters and just as we were settling in before the national anthems, the two remaining seats right in front of us were filled by a couple. The woman was maybe seven months pregnant, maybe even a little more. Her whole belly had been used as a canvas. Proudly displayed beneath a tank top and above hipster jeans – a hemisphere of Mexican skin with three colours of body paint!!! Could we say – very much a nava(e)l occasion!

The Angolan team were underdogs and yet they played with incredible composure on the ball, I thought. Possibly tactics designed to frustrate the Mexicans who showed little in the way of trying to handle the problems that Angola posed. The Mexicans were clearly a good side and whilst much of their play was skilful they could not penetrate the Angolan defence well enough to create really clear chances. Angola still found the time to attack and did so with a certain amount of verve.

It was an absorbing encounter and was one of those games, the enjoyment of which remains a mystery to Australian Rules football fans, the 0-0 draw.

For all the resilience and organisation of the Angolans, my friend alongside pondered what conceding a goal would do to Angola's composure. I was not so sure they would fold. Their goalkeeper played exceptionally well, extremely sound in his work but also in directing his team.

It was not to be a goal conceded which would test the Angolans, but the loss of a player sent off by the referee. This left them around 15 minutes to survive with 10 men. For Mexico, we can say they went close, but no cigar!

The real hero for Angola was the goalkeeper, João Ricardo, one of two players from a Portuguese background (the other being Figueiredo). Ricardo was rock solid and also pulled off a couple top saves to deny Mexico, and deservedly received the Man of the Match award.

Group D – Third match

18 June 2006, FIFA World Cup Stadium (AWD Arena), Hanover

Mexico   0 : 0   Angola

Referee: Shamsul Maidin (Singapore)

Attendance: 43,000

CHAPTER SIX
6:52AM TRAIN BERLIN TO MUNICH

Next I was off to Munich for Australia's game against Brazil. The match kicked off at 6:00pm Munich time and I wanted to see a bit of Munich and leave myself time to find a spot at the Fan Fest site. It's a six hour plus journey so I took the 6:52am train from Berlin main station – and left home at 5:45am for the bike ride to Lichterfelde West S Bahn station.

I wondered whether 'Son of Stan,' Jack the ticket man, would materialise at some point on the journey, and what would I pay if I was offered a ticket for the game? When I bought my ticket for the Japan game I asked the tout if he had tickets for the Brazil game too, and he had indicated a price of 650 Euros! I wasn't going to pay that.

I reserved a seat on the train the night before, which I thought was a good idea as they still allowed smoking in designated carriages. Not reserving a seat could leave you with the only vacant seat being in such a carriage. Are you one of those people for whom it seems that no matter where you are standing in a line for tickets or waiting to enter a venue, people wanting to cross that line always cut across you? I am.

I know there are statistical theories and techniques about queuing, so maybe there is a 'Picken's Law' I don't know about. The same thing happens in a no smoking zone. If there is a surreptitious smoker, I always seem to get the seat next to them. Why me, in a grandstand of some 15,000? You sniff that tell-tale pungent waft in your nostrils, and you look around. There it is, right next to you, the bloke has the ciggie in the reverse hold, the lit end pointing towards his palm like a 14-year-old sneaking a drag behind the school bike shed. I'd had this happen a couple of times already.

I felt sure I read somewhere in a missive from Franz Beckenbauer, who was head of the Organising Committee, that for the World Cup they had made all stadiums no smoking zones.

On one occasion, not wishing to cause a scene I waited until half time and then cobbled together enough Spanish to tell the guy next to me that smoking was not allowed. No luck there, so I then tried to catch the attention of the stadium staff. First bloke was a security guard who was having a drag himself! I then spoke to a volunteer, "I don't like it either," he said. "But I don't think it is disallowed." I returned to my seat after a 20 minute respite and as I settled in, the video screen displayed a flashing sign – the lit cigarette image inside the red circle with a red stripe across it, and the slogan, "Thank you for not smoking!"

At the Berlin Olympic Stadium, I spotted one guy having a smoke at half-time – he was completely oblivious to the 'No Smoking' sign pinned to the wall directly above his head!

I am reminded of flights quite a few years back when there used to be smoking and no smoking zones on aeroplanes. It was always possible that you could get a seat that was right on the dividing line, and it made sod all difference to your air quality if there was a chorus of smokers on the first row of the smoking area. It's a bit like that when you get this 'soddit I'm having a smoke' type sitting next to you.

Diego Maradona could be spotted on the TV coverage at many games. A couple of times I'd seen him puffing on a cigar. Obviously, the rule doesn't apply to the Hand of God – or maybe just not in hospitality boxes.

(OR HOW I SPENT MY LONG SERVICE LEAVE)

My train journey as far as Fulda was uneventful. Fulda is a town I had not heard of before I came to Germany for this trip. It seemed to be a hub of sorts for the railway system. If you were comparing it with the UK, you would say it's like Crewe.

I wonder if its football team has a name as distinguished as the Alexandra? I changed in Fulda for a train to Nuremburg and from there another train to Munich. When you were on the move like this you almost always saw fans from other nations. Sometimes they were from countries in your group and sometimes from others; changing trains and making their connections to another World Cup venue city.

Australia was to play Brazil in the new World Cup stadium (Allianz Arena) in Munich. From the photos the stadium had the look of a neat bundle of clothing contained in a hair net. Not exactly sure, but I do believe the enclosing walls and roof (what we call the envelope in the construction business) were entirely fabric stretched across a frame – the sort of style I have only seen used for stadium roofing before.

The other game in our group that day was Japan vs Croatia and there were groups of each country's supporters on Fulda's platform four. They were due to play in Nuremberg, kicking off three hours before we did. Supporters of each country were greeting each other and wishing them luck. There was an almost unspoken bond between us – "We have travelled all this way to see and support our heroes, because we love this game and so have you. All in all, we are the same." I am sorry if that sounds trite, but I really believe that is about the size of it.

The Japan Croatia game would be finished before ours started and my plan called for a Japanese win as I thought that would finish off Croatia. Surely, Brazil would beat Japan on 22nd June – the day of the final group matches deciding which teams would go forward into the knockout phase of the competition.

A win for Japan that day would leave us knowing that a draw with Brazil ought to be enough. A win against Brazil would be lovely but maybe a bit too ambitious to imagine against the World Champs.

My daughter, Leila, was to come over from London for Australia's final group game against Croatia as we both had tickets. Legitimate tickets I should add.

I knew that a win or bust situation would be exhilarating – in an Australia versus Uruguay sort of way. It was bright and sunny in Fulda and I took it as a good sign that from a flagpole visible above the station roof, the flags of just Germany and Australia fluttered in the breeze.

I arrived in Munich. 'Jack' hadn't showed up and so I didn't have to face the question of how much I would pay. I made my way to the Fan Fest area which was located in the 1972 Olympic stadium precinct. I thought it was only the Olympic stadium that had the acrylic glass tented roof structure, but I found that many of the facilities, the gymnastics hall, for example, have a similar construction. It's very striking and supported with what can only be called long guy ropes swooping down from under each roof and off some considerable distance away from the structure and anchored in massive concrete blocks.

The actual Fan Fest area sat between the Olympic stadium and other Olympic venues, along a sort of concourse. Falling away from this was a huge amphitheatre overlooking a lake. At the lakeside there was a huge video screen and the seating bowl had been extended to accommodate 35,000. Together with the people on the concourse and others round about there must have been upwards of 50,000 people there.

(OR HOW I SPENT MY LONG SERVICE LEAVE)

As I made my way from the security area past the restaurant and beer tents I saw a very familiar sight. You may have seen through email circulars from friends, pictures of the joke football pitch laid out on a steep hillside complete with goals. I think it was circulated as a mickey take of some competition or other (Athens Olympics? Not sure), where problems were reported with progress and quality of construction work. Well, this pitch is actually in Olympic Park in Munich. There it was. The joke pitch on the hillside on the far side of the lake beyond the Fan Fest amphitheatre. So, a quick snap of that one.

As I wandered around the area waiting for the Japan vs Croatia game, I started to get the feeling that there were a lot of expat Aussies in Germany for the World Cup. That is, Aussies living in, say, London, who were over for the World Cup. In some cases just for one or two games or even no games. It was as if there was a, "We're over here in Europe, mate, this could be a once in a lifetime opportunity. No tickets? Who cares? Get over there; be a part of it." I mean you would ,wouldn't you?

In more than a few cases they were not football people, you can pick it up from the conversation as you breeze by. It's not really the comments like, "Get the ball towards our goal!" Actually they mean the opposition's goal; the one we are attacking – opposite terminology to Australian Rules Football. In soccer, that is, real football, "our goal" is the one we are defending. Nonetheless, they are Australian and they wanted to be there and all the best to them.

One beauty I saw was to do with the desire to wear something Aussie in terms of team clothing. You have got to wear something with which you clearly advertise your allegiance. Of course, the ideal was a replica jersey of what the Socceroos were wearing. There were variations on this theme – an actual replica of the World Cup 2006 jersey being the premier choice, and then you got the different versions of the Socceroos jersey over the years. There were many of the type worn in the play-off against Uruguay; you even saw some from the time we played Iran in 1997.

Of course, there was the Green and Gold Army commemorative jersey from 1974 which I wore. Then there were also the folks that didn't have anything in the way of a football jersey. Thus, you saw Wallabies jerseys or one-day cricket shirts. Later on that day after the game, I even saw a lad in the centre of Munich wearing the jumper of my hometown Australian Rules football team, the Geelong Cats. It was topped off with an Aussie flag as a cape. Anything that loudly proclaims who you belong to.

The best one was a lad over from London who clearly, like the rest of us, was anxious to show his colours. All he had to his name was an Australian one-day cricket shirt, you can almost imagine it was a case of, "Oh, bugger it, it will have to do." There he was among the throng, singing along, and emblazoned across his back, 'BOON'! I thought how totally appropriate? A David Boon cricket shirt, at a time when the amber fluid was flowing in a torrent? Boon, it is said, is the holder of the record for consuming the most beer on the flight from Australia going to London for an Ashes tour.

With some of the venue cities the Fan Fest was often not far from the main stadium or on the way to it. Examples would be Kaiserslautern (very close) and Stuttgart (visit the Fan Fest and then take the train from the nearby station to the stadium). In Munich, the World Cup stadium was in a different part of town and there was no obvious need or prompt to go to both. As such there was no-one that I saw roaming the Fan Fest area, with placards, 'Anyone need tickets' or carrying the plaintive, 'I need tickets' or *Suchen karten* (searching for tickets).

(OR HOW I SPENT MY LONG SERVICE LEAVE)

Once you were at the Fan Fest area you had pretty well decided that was where you were going to be – and you were not really in the market for the 'funny' tickets. So, folks just get on with the revelry.

There were supporters of all four Group F nations in the Fan Fest, but by far the most numerous were the Brazilians and before long a samba band started up.

I'd never heard one close up. The basic idea seems to be continuous rhythmic drumming - and loud. Pretty soon a big crowd within the immediate vicinity of the band was dancing – there were the colours of each nation, bobbing, swaying, rocking and a'rolling. It may not have been Mardi Gras in Rio, but it was quite a sight.

Japan and Croatia played out a goalless draw. Japan went close to scoring on a couple of occasions and Croatia had their share of chances.

That made it clear for us. We assume Brazil will beat Japan in the final game – and if they don't then it will be the biggest boilover since ... well, to put it bluntly, there hasn't been a boilover like it.

Therefore, it made no difference what happened between us and Brazil, a draw with Croatia on the coming Thursday would see us qualify as second in the group for the knockout phase of the tournament.

We knew we could achieve this, it was just that the majority of the footballing world did not. They seem to be blind to the fact that our players operate in their normal playing lives in what are among the top national competitions in the world – the English Premier League, *Serie* A in Italy and *La Liga* in Spain. We have a couple playing in Switzerland – but the Swiss national team were in this World Cup, so nothing to be ashamed of there.

CHAPTER SEVEN

YOUR WOMEN ARE GREAT

I have this love hate relationship with Brazil. I have admitted on many occasions, I am hopelessly in love with the way they play football. They, in turn, are in love with the ball itself, and that is why they play the way they do. Not to have possession of the ball is a violation of their senses. With either foot they caress the ball, they stroke it. It is theirs and they will not give it up without a fight.

My problem is, when my teams play them and stand up to them, and show some skill too, I want our skill to be recognised alongside theirs. They are wonderfully talented, but ball skills are not their exclusive preserve. In short, I want to beat them. All too often, it doesn't work out that way. You could rarely, if ever, call the Brazilians lucky but just sometimes they seem to get the rub of the green, as it were. I don't know what it is. I guess if you are that good you make your own luck.

It happened on the day Australia played them in Munich. We really held our own, I thought, and had plenty of chances to score but it just wouldn't happen for us. Mark Viduka, Harry Kewell, and Mark Bresciano all had chances.

The Bresciano effort was a case in point. Deep into the second half, we were one down and the ball bounced into the Brazil six yard box – Bresciano, with a swivel, launched himself to a horizontal position, and with a scissor like kick, got good purchase on the ball goalwards, but it flew too close to the keeper. He probably hit it too well – a slight error or mis-hit may have fooled the goalie, but it was not to be.

(OR HOW I SPENT MY LONG SERVICE LEAVE)

Then in the dying stages Brazil on the attack, a shot from the right, close in, struck Schwarzer's near post. True, he was beaten, but it goes into the books as off target. The rebound could have gone anywhere – but where did it go? It fell invitingly to the incoming Brazilian player, Fred – he could have got down on his knees and blown it in. My grannie could have notched with that one.

One of my main beefs is with commentators who drool over the Brazilians. True, they are prime drooling material, but what I don't like is that commentators fail to similarly recognise the same skill level in players of other countries. The effort by Bresciano, goal or no goal, would have been shown in replay after replay had it been produced by Ronaldinho (at that time the world's best player and a man of incredible skill – witness the Nike TV advert where he, quite intentionally and repeatedly, kicks the ball against the crossbar from 18 yards – or was it trick photography?).

Joe Cole, for England, scored a stunning goal against Sweden in a Group B match. Hit from almost 30 metres out, the ball swerved and dipped on its missile like course for the top right hand corner of the goal. Totally premeditated and produced in an instant from a dropping ball that his body movement manufactured into the chance to volley as it dropped (thus producing the viciously dipping, swerving arc as it neared the goal). That, ladies and gentlemen, was skill of the highest order. There was a moment or two of delirium from the German commentator but then it was gone. Not sure what the BBC made of it. It must surely have made it into the highlights DVD of this World Cup.

In Germany, the whole country and a goodly few of the non-Brazilian visitors are involved in the same Brazil worship. In Munich, at the Fan Fest there were some 50,000 people for the Australia vs Brazil game. We were outnumbered by three to one, at least, maybe more. We didn't have the samba bands but a great job was made of singing *Advance Australia Fair*. Incidentally, how do you get those big drums on an aeroplane within the baggage allowance? One Australian chant I heard was, "Your football's shite but your women are great!!" Erm… correct in one assertion only!!

The odd thing was that as many of these 'Brazilian'"supporters passed by me they were speaking German. Now I know there are reputed to be some Germans holed up in South America but not that many! At that time anything with the remotest connection to Brazil was the biggest ticket in town. They would have got record sales for a mixed box of yellow and green paper clips I'm sure. "Get on board!" was the catch cry. I don't think the notion of supporting the underdog was a big part of life in Germany. Anyone could be a Brazil supporter. Buy the shirt; make like you can samba.

Tickets to all of their games were at an absolute premium. For official purposes, I guess all games were pretty much sold out. That is to say, the tickets have been bought from the World Cup organisers at source. We have already established, though, that tickets could be found, it's just a question of what you were prepared to pay. For a Brazil ticket for a game against the most ignominious of opposition you would pay a fortune. Goodness knows what the correct analogy is … maybe ask yourself what you would have paid if, before John Lennon died, the Beatles had ever got back together for a concert. Brazil are that big.

There were examples of the "Brazil phenomenon" being used to great effect. I visited an exhibition called Pelé Station in Berlin's *Potsdamer Platz*. They actually changed the signage at one of the Platz's railway station entrances.

"Pelé Station" it says across the archway and inside there was an exhibition to celebrate the great man. Pelé, of course, being the legendary Brazilian player of the late 1950s through to the mid-70s – 1,366 games for 1,281 goals – incomprehensible numbers.

To compare – for baseball, think of Barry Bonds, Hank Aaron, or Babe Ruth belting, say, 1000 career home runs (their totals were in the 700s). For cricket, think of Sachin Tendulkar scoring perhaps 20,000 test match runs (he actually amassed 15,921). In Australian Rules Football, think about Jason Dunstall (actual 1,254) or Tony Lockett (actual 1,360) scoring over 2000 goals in their careers; and you will get a feel for this man's achievements.

We should add though that Pelé's stats include friendly games and those when he was in the armed services. Whilst there are three other football players who exceed his career totals Pelé's numbers are massive. Add to his goalscoring feats the fact that he was a man with the most prodigious of skills with any legitimate part of the body. He was an innovator – no-one before him had used the chest to pass the ball. He is credited with inventing the bicycle kick. More precisely, the upside down bicycle kick!!

It is perhaps almost poetic that a moment of incredible athleticism and skill from Pelé during the 1970 World Cup in Mexico produced not a goal but, what is agreed by many as, the greatest save ever seen from a goalkeeper, namely England's Gordon Banks. I pretty much recall the words of BBC commentator, David Coleman, on that day. It went something like, "Well... that is extraordinary... Gordon Banks has literally conjured the ball out of the net!!" So certain a goal would appear.

Excuse me if I blaspheme but seeing the Pelé artefacts in this exhibition was almost like, if not actually like, viewing religious relics. There are two pairs of his boots; the ball with which he scored his 1000th goal; his World Cup winner's medals, the only player with three and, oddly, they are not grand pieces of jewellery in any way at all; his ID credentials for the 1966 and 1970 World Cup tournaments.

The IDs are really low key, like an old club membership card, not the dangle round your neck, outsize, "Look at me, look at me... look at the size of my tournament ID... I'm important," things of today. Quaintly, the 1966 one is endorsed, "Free admission to stadiums. Standing enclosure only." "What's thee name, lad?" I can almost hear a north country Englishman on the turnstile saying, "Yer what? 'Pelley' is it? Owright lad, well thee can stand over there for a minute or two."

Something I learned at the exhibition was that Pelé scored his 1000th goal on the day that Conrad and Bean (Apollo 12) made the second landing on the Moon. I knew that the various moon landings must have been in the same era, so to speak, but so coincident?! They shared the front pages of the world's newspapers the following day.

In this exhibition, Pelé was using his own reputation and a bit of the Brazil hype for charity purposes. He and his people had set up the exhibition to raise funds to go to Pelé's support for severely underprivileged children in Brazil.

CHAPTER EIGHT

OH, YES!!!

Let's get into it straight away – you will know the, "Oh yes!!!" of my title refers to the fantastic effort by the Socceroos in their final group game to reach the Round of Sixteen.

Twice the boys came back from a goal deficit to square the match for the draw they needed to progress at the expense of Croatia, their opponents. They would now meet Italy in Kaiserslautern (scene of our opening 3-1 win over Japan) in yet another clash with one of Australia's major migrant cultures. Just as against Croatia, there would be ethnic representatives in the Australian squad for the Italy game – Mark Viduka, Josip Skoko among those from a Croatian background.

Interestingly enough, there were three boys in the Croatia squad who were also born in Australia and chose to pursue their international careers in the land of their parents.

In the game against Italy, we would have Mark Bresciano (half Croatian too actually) and Vince Grella making the cultural connection. Unfortunately, the international career of Christian Vieri was over or we would have had on Italy's side a player who spent a good deal of his young life in Sydney. Vieri fancied himself as a fast bowler,and numbers Steve Waugh among his sporting heroes.

Sadly, Brett Emerton would miss the Italy clash having been sent off in the Croatia game. Referee Graham Poll ejected Emerton after having to book him for the second time in the game.

In compiling my diary I was running out of superlatives. The success of the tournament as an event, never mind the football being played, was clearly the result of some very thoughtful and detailed planning on the part of the organisers. However, this could only be part of the story. True, the organisers must have put in place many, many ideas – among them the free Fan Fests in each city to allow those without tickets to enjoy the games at the next best level with huge video screens – sometimes multiple screens – plus all the fun of the fair with the drink, food tents, face painting, and souvenir shops.

At the other end was the incredible logistics of the security effort – all done diligently, yet thoroughly with bag checks and body searches for everyone entering a match stadium. Let's not suggest the folks on security duties are normally impolite people, but clearly there had been a big effort on training – one theme of which must have been something like, "We can do this properly without being Mr and Mrs Grumpy."

Today, as I cleared security at the stadium, my security man was smiling. Opened every pocket of my small rucksack, checked every nook and cranny and then, said, "Thank you, now, please close your bag here so that you do not lose anything. Here, I can help you ... please enjoy the game." This closing of the search takes but a few seconds and goes a long way, in my view, to making you feel the search was necessary but not overly intrusive.

The police, as ever, were in evidence, as they are everywhere and in numbers. The authorities left nothing to chance, and it was reported that huge numbers of police have been brought into the World Cup venue cities from other areas. They operate in teams and each one includes women officers, presumably so that decorum prevails should there be a need to deal with the female side of the crowds. They seem both diligent and vigilant. Clearly, there was a seriousness in

(OR HOW I SPENT MY LONG SERVICE LEAVE)

their demeanour (which was only reasonable), but the most trying assignments I had seen to date were for the female officers posing for photographs with the overseas visitors.

The fans played their part too by arriving early at stadiums and, pretty well universally, being well behaved. It all helped. The whole event, though seemed to take on a life of its own. Dare I say it, Sydney 2000 style? It has gripped the nation, and if BBC World TV was anything to go by it was gripping the planet too.

Stories from home in Australia confirmed the same – cold weather not dampening the spirits of thousands in Federation Square, Melbourne and, no doubt, in similar gathering places.

Naturally, the performance of the Socceroos fired that enthusiasm. In each venue city the "fest effect," spreads out from the Fan Fest location itself to nearby bars, restaurants, and squares. If you had a match ticket you could go to your venue city, take in an earlier game at the Fan Fest; eat, drink, be merry, enjoy the football and, as we were urged by the tournament motto, take the 'time to make friends.' Lots of photographs were taken by the visitors, of each person, of each group that was travelling together, of groups that were ad hoc. Fans of opposing teams get talking and before long there was a photo. If you had a dollar for every time you saw people, who clearly have never met before, taking group photos or for someone answering the call, "Could you take a picture for us?" you would be a wealthy person.

There were street performers and pavements artists temporarily memorialising the players in coloured chalk. At 1 o'clock in the morning after the game, there was a guy doing tricks on a pogo stick in Stuttgart's *Schlossplatz* – leaping over two audience participants as they lay on the ground. There was a guy who fancies his chances on the chess board, and he was taking on all comers two at a time. What do you want? Man playing a saxophone with a parrot on his head? Oh yeah, we had one of those – honest!! A samba band started up with rhythmic, loud drumming and the crowd nearby started jigging.

Then there were the volunteers. In recent times, the heroes of almost every major sporting event have been the volunteers and World Cup 2006 was no exception. These guys (and that's not a gender specific term) really were a delight. Bilingualism was a key skill as you might expect (their own language plus German) and they have come from all corners of the globe. Many were émigrés living in Germany and, on going to pick up my daughter's ticket for the game, we had a personal guide from Stuttgart station. "Please come with me, I'm going to start my shift," said the Brazilian lady who had lived in Germany for 25 years.

We chatted – "I have a friend who lives in Porto Alegre," I said. "So Gremio are my team."

She replied, "I am from São Paulo and I support Santos, the team of Pelé."

Before each match a stadium announcer went pitch-side to welcome the crowd and announce the players and part of the routine was to pull in volunteers from one or both of the countries about to take the field. They were almost always an extrovert and that day a lad from Melbourne who lived in Germany got the gig. "Australia, welcome to Stuttgart!!"

Cheers reverberated around the stadium and then he led the assembled yellow clad multitude in, "Aussie, Aussie, Aussie," "Oi, oi, oi," came back the reply. He had the easiest job in the world!!

My daughter flew in to Frankfurt from London just for the Croatia game. Beside herself with excitement and all her friends around the world vicariously

(OR HOW I SPENT MY LONG SERVICE LEAVE)

so. "Leila, I ca-n-not believe you will be going to the game!!"

We met at the main station, me having come in from Berlin, and then took the train to Stuttgart in the afternoon.

We arrived in Stuttgart and made our way to the Fan Fest in the *SchlossPlatz*, a huge city centre garden in front of the palace – just a five minute walk from the main station. There were thousands of people. By far, the majority were in Croatian colours which comprised variations on the theme of that part of the Croatian flag which is red and white checks.

There were the Croatia replica jerseys, which were fully red and white checks. ("Your shirt ... is like a table cloth," chanted the Aussies, to the tune of Village People's, *Go West!*). There were people with full tailored suits in the red and white check, women in tight fitting dresses in red and white check. Flat caps, floppy caps, umbrellas – all in red and white checks. There were sprinklings of Aussie colours here and there and finally, as we reached the square proper, we saw that the green and gold had colonised a whole corner.

In amongst them, there are Croatian colours to be seen. At the other end, occupying a huge area of the steps are the massed ranks of red and white. We were going to be outnumbered today for sure, just like we were in Munich for the Brazil game. This mingling of the fans would have been a cause for concern in times gone by. In fact, it would have been strictly disallowed by the authorities.

What we had, though, was a coming together that was exhilarating to see. There were the joint photo opportunities I've already mentioned, but there were groups travelling together with some members wearing red and white and others green and gold, and some a bit of both. There are people with a Socceroos jersey and a Croatia scarf; a Croatia jersey and an Australia cap.

THE TIME OF MY FOOTBALL LIFE

Yet others have created a half and half jersey or a half and half scarf.

We met an Australian family on the train to the stadium. Mum was wearing a Croatia shirt, Dad and kids wearing Australia shirts with the kids topping off the look with a Croatia flag. The whole family had come to Germany with just one match ticket each and they were looking for the scalpers to supply the tickets for the game.

The football in the whole tournament was good. At that stage there had been 44 games and 110 goals at an average of two and a half. Only five of those games had been goalless. For the uninitiated, this is just a tad below average – there had only been one blow out score. There are no disproportionately weak teams.

They all played with composure on the ball and largely accurate passing, and the key was do not offer the opposition an easy chance to regain possession. It is easy to knock this and say that all teams had reached at least a level that produced boring, colourless competence. This, though, is a view that seeks to consign football's developing nations to the naivety that often resulted in them being cannon fodder. Holders of such views long for the errant silliness of, for example, Zaire in 1974, when Germany last hosted the World Cup. By 2006, high quality coaching had given these countries more organisation, more composure. Every team possessed its stars that could produce moments of prodigious skill, stunning shots and wonderful goals. So, all teams are competitive when they have possession of the ball.

From my observations, the real differences appear with the, stronger, more advanced nations who distinguish themselves by being extremely competitive when they do not have the ball. If an opponent gains possession in his half or in the midfield, the top teams do not fall back; they contest the ball right there

(OR HOW I SPENT MY LONG SERVICE LEAVE)

high up the field. This was very good football.

The Gottlieb Daimler Stadium is a beauty. It neatly and comfortably accommodates the supporters, though not extravagantly so. As with all the stadia – some completely new and for others a major refurb – the key was the edifice as a piece of sculpture. A major element in Stuttgart was a beam encircling the stadium high above the roof line looking like a distorted hula hoop and from which the roof is suspended – very distinctive.

We entered our zone and before finding our seats, partake of bratwurst on a bread roll which really hits the spot. I recalled the quip of one my English friends who, remarking on the small bread roll and the huge size of the sausage overhanging each end, said, "All these years and they still haven't invented a bread roll to fit the sausage!"

As we took our seats I introduced myself to my neighbour, Terry from Sydney who, like myself, was a veteran of the previous November's qualifier against Uruguay at Sydney's Olympic Stadium. We speculated on whether the Croatia game was bigger than Uruguay. In some sense it was. There are not 80,000 Australians here but there are huge numbers and it was, perhaps, yet another step forward for football in Australia. If we draw, we would be into uncharted waters – beyond the group stage for the first time ever.

The late Johnny Warren, the great champion of Australian football, would have been a proud man were he still with us.

Terry had come to Germany with two match tickets – one for the Japan game purchased in Sydney from a 'well known' football coach of his acquaintance, plus this Croatia match ticket that like ours, came through Football Federation Australia ballot. (The Japan ticket was also through FFA, of course, but indirectly, if you catch my drift!) He had also managed to snag a ticket for the Brazil game in Munich on match day – 450 Euro for a 100 Euro ticket.

My immediate task was to find a spot for my 'Surf Coast FC, Torquay Australia' banner. Some of the stadiums had not been designed with banner hanging in mind. We were about ten rows back on the upper tier, but there was a short rail at the front row position of our aisle. Tailor made. Great position, directly opposite the players' tunnel and opposite the media boxes and everyone around admired the banner, our club colours with blue letters on a yellow background. I thought that if there was someone from SBS-TV assigned to use the binoculars to scan the stadium for good shots and ask the local TV people to give them a go, surely we would get a bit on telly, but I don't think it happened.

My next job was to take a photo, but how to get to the lower tier and shoot it? Enter our wonderful volunteers. I explain what I would like, and this lovely woman offered to take me to the lower tier, an area for which I did not have a ticket, and cleared it with the security guard, so that I could shoot upwards with my back to the pitch. Not the slightest doubt or sharp intake of breath. "Of course, it's my pleasure."

The players came out for the warm up and immediately the talk turned to speculation on what will be our starting XI. The pattern was for the whole squad to come out and initially they are all engaged in the same warm up routine. Eventually, though, you could work out who was going to start. The selected ten outfield players started to work together, Mark Bresciano was not among them, but Tim Cahill and Harry Kewell were. Our coach Guus Hiddink was a man who thought deeply about his selections – it was no reflection on a player not to be starting. He seems to choose players, not because they might do something

(OR HOW I SPENT MY LONG SERVICE LEAVE)

individually brilliant, but because collectively they made up the shape of what he believed was needed for the occasion. He is a master tactician.

As for the goalies, the goalkeeping coach, Tony Franken, works with the three keepers separately, and they with each other, in the warm up. Eventually, he works more intensively with the man chosen. It was Zeljko Kalac! Mark Schwarzer had been between the sticks in our other two games. He seemed to be running freely, so why had Guus chosen 'Spider' Kalac?

The warm up concluded and a short time later the players returned, resplendent in the match kit, for the anthems, coin toss, and exchange of souvenirs. What we in the crowd may have lacked in numbers we made up for in volume of sound. The rendition of *Advance Australia Fair* was among the most moving I have heard. It was almost as if we knew, intuitively, that it must be extra loud to give the boys a lift.

The match started and before we are even settled a free kick was awarded against Mark Viduka. Pretty innocuous, I thought, but the referee, Graham Poll of England, adjudges it a trip on the Croatian skipper Niko Kovač. Up stepped right wing back Darijo Srna and curled in a superb free kick from 25 metres – brilliantly weighted to get up and over the wall but then dipping down leaving Kalac groping fresh air. Damn!!

However, the Australian side roar back, step up a gear, and then control the game for long periods. Kewell, Cahill, and Culina all went close. Then a cross from the right was handled by Croatia's Stjepan Tomas. Referee Poll seemed to agonise like Steve Bucknor making an L.B.W. decision but awarded Australia a penalty kick which Craig Moore converted comfortably. The Aussie crowd went wild – we were hugging people we had never met before, my specs went flying in the celebration.

THE TIME OF MY FOOTBALL LIFE

We were level! A draw was all Australia needed to progress; we just had to keep it that way at least. Specs recovered, we then saw out the half with few problems. Ominously, Kalac fumbled a corner but no danger ensued.

Croatia returned for the second half in a much more positive style and started to exert some pressure. Then, in the 56th minute Kovac sent in a weak, seemingly harmless low shot. Kalac went down and for a second seemed to have it covered. Then, in an instant, horror of horrors, the ball appeared to squirm through and over his body all at once. 2 – 1 to Croatia. The Australians in the crowd were speechless. Why on earth did Guus not select Schwarzer in goal, what must he have been thinking?

The Australians seemed to redouble their efforts. Hiddink again took a hand, making bold substitutions, bringing on attackers for defenders or midfielders. The problem was that Stipe Pletikosa, the Croatian goalkeeper, started to play out of his skin and made several brilliant saves. In particular, an instinctive parry from a point blank blast from Kewell was breathtaking.

Just when it seemed the ball would not go in, Kewell latched on to a flick from John Aloisi, drove it across Pletikosa and into the goal. Delirium unrestrained!! Surely we had made it.

There were still some eleven minutes plus three of additional time to go, but Australia held on for a famous result.

Both teams ended the game without full teams. Towards the end, in quick succession, both Dario Simić and Brett Emerton received second yellow cards in separate incidents, leaving Poll no option but to show the red card and dismiss them.

In a strange incident, Australian born-and-bred Croatian player Josip Simunic

(OR HOW I SPENT MY LONG SERVICE LEAVE)

was dismissed right near the end under the two yellow equals a red card rule. The odd thing was that Simunic may be the only player ever to be booked (shown the yellow card) three times. Referee Poll, as well as being mathematically challenged, presumably suffered from a touch of the, "Well, all these names sound the same don't they?" affliction.

Apparently, Mark Viduka got a flea in his ear from Poll earlier for pointing out that he had booked the player before when the second yellow card was produced for Simunic. Stick to shirt numbers from now on Graham! I expect there were some interesting chants at English football grounds when Poll resumed duty the following season.

The game ended in mild confusion with referee Poll seeming to have blown for a free kick, but before the game could restart he obviously returned the whistle to his mouth to end the game. In the cacophony of noise no-one heard it and as the referee stepped forward to collect the ball, the Australian players realised it was all over. They were through to the Round of Sixteen to play Italy the following Monday.

After the final whistle there followed fully 20 minutes of singing by the Australian supporters with hardly any leaving the stadium. It was as if an Australian had captured the public address control room and plugged in his or her iPod! We had Mark Seymour, ACker DaCker, and then there was bit of Bon Jovi thrown in.

When the players returned after a few minutes to salute their fans, the floor beneath us was shaking with the jumping up and down, and the stadium was reverberating to the sound of everyone singing along to Men at Work's Down Under. As the players trooped along the touchline they picked up on the beat and, hands high in the air, were clapping along with the crowd. A memorable moment among many.

As I joked with the guy at a sportswear shop a few days earlier as we looked at his paltry stock of Australian jerseys against racks full of other countries. "I'm not sure it's a question of being sold out of Aussie stuff. I reckon you didn't order enough in the first place. You are not taking us seriously!!"

Maybe now they would.

As we left the Gottlieb Daimler stadium after the Croatia game and Australia's place in the Round of Sixteen secured, we saw for the first time people with placards indicating that they were 'Collecting used tickets.' What on earth for? Collectors' items for offering on eBay? Forging tickets for future games? Great reaction from an Aussie lad, as he breezed past these people, "No, no, no ... thank you," he almost chanted. "I am going to frame it and look at it a lot!!"

Group F Final match

22 June 2006, Gottlieb Daimler Stadium, Stuttgart

Croatia 2 : 2 Australia

Srna 2' Moore 38' (pen)

N. Kovac 56' Kewell 79'

Referee: Graham Poll (England)

Attendance: 52,000

CHAPTER NINE
TESTING GERMANY

Germany pumped up the pressure even more on 20th June, beating Ecuador 3-0 in their final group game at the Berlin Olympic Stadium. The German team were staying in Berlin, five minutes by car up the road from where I stayed. This match was the game for the home team in the capital. A sell out in the 70-odd thousand seater stadium, but the big statistic was a reported 750,000 at the Fan Fest, which runs from the Brandenburg Gate along the length of 17th June Street.

This was where I watched the game and it was quite a sight and experience. The so-called Fan Miele (Fan Mile) was just the best thing for this public TV viewing caper. In Berlin, the main stage and screen, the Fan Fest site, was immediately in front of the Brandenburg Gate on the (old) West side. Down the whole Fan Mile, the avenue stretching away from the Gate, you found video screens, strung back to back high above the road level, perhaps every 80 to 100 metres, and in front of each there were benches and sometimes tables on which to rest your beer and bratwurst. If you didn't have a ticket for the stadium, this was the way to watch football!!

The Germans thought they were on a roll to win this thing and the population was reacting accordingly. Chanting, singing, blowing whistles, sounding car horns. Anything which made a noise. Even away from the official areas - the stadium and the Fan Fest - there was a carnival atmosphere.

In a square in the heart of Berlin's shopping area there was a concert stage, wall to wall food and drink stalls. Accredited World Cup volunteers were there to answer your questions with a smile. Video screens a plenty and these areas were jammed at match times.

As for Germany's chances, it's true the team was showing a bit of that distinctive quality of peaking at the right time after having an indifferent year or two. As hosts, Germany did not have to qualify. No nerve-wracking penalty shoot-out against Uruguay for them.

Their last competitive tournament was the European Championships in 2004, when they went out at the group stages with two draws and one loss. I had a suspicion they had not been really tested yet at World Cup 2006. They had a fairly easy group and in the previous day's (the last) group game, once the first goal went in, Ecuador seemed to reduce to a stroll in the full knowledge they were already through to the next stage.

Germany was due to play Sweden in the Round of Sixteen. The Swedes, likewise, entered their last group game against England knowing there was no need for exertion. Two of their star players, Henrik Larrson and Zlatan Ibrahimović, had yet to switch on the turbo in the tournament and could give the German defence its first stern examination. If Germany got past Sweden, likely to be waiting for them might be Argentina who were due to play Mexico.

Argentina had come to the tournament among, if not as, the favourites. Only then, I fancied, would we see whether this German team was the real deal.

England Supporters' banners in the stadium at Frankfurt for England's opening game. They really are amongst the best at this caper.

Our banner. Just as parochial as any England Fan!

Football? A poster in a Frankfurt shop window showing Australian Rules football players. No I cannot explain it.

Spot the ball - England supporters take over a Frankfurt square.

The ticket I bought on the train to Kaiserslautern from "Jack" The hidden ID number would presumably be held in FFA records and, along with the barcode, could identify the source. That is, to whom FFA legitimately passed the ticket but who, in turn, illegitimately passed the ticket on to the black market.

Business card of a ticket scalper - Details hidden to protect... erm to protect me!!!

The two teams from my home city in the United Kingdom; Port Vale and Stoke City. Usually bitter enemies, but here united in one cause - supporting England at the World Cup. (Five points if you can guess the song title hinted at in the flag slogan).

The Brazilian way!

Mexican Bike!!

A legitimate ticket allocated to me by the Football Association in England — the only body in the world not to have the country name in the title, presumably because it was the first such association. I am a member of the official supporters association — England Fans. Only members of England Fans could legitimately obtain tickets from the official allocation which the Football Association received from FIFA. England Fans made the allocation by ballot and also on the basis of the number of England matches, if any, a member had attended before the allocation took place. It was collected in Germany from England Fans representatives.

A legitimate ticket allocated to me by the Ticket Shop of the official World Cup website. It is personalised with my name. The ticket was collected by me in person (as required) and printed on Sunday, 11th June 2006, at the ticket Collection Point near the Olympic Stadium in Berlin.

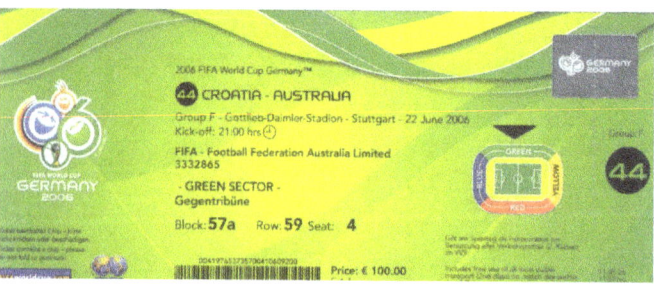

A legitimate ticket allocated to me by FFA or, to be more precise, by FFA's agents FFA Travel (aka The Fanatics). The ID number beneath the words 'FIFA — Football Federation Australia' should make it possible to trace the ticket back to me. Collected in person at FFA Travel's pick up point at Frankfurt Airport's Sheraton Hotel.

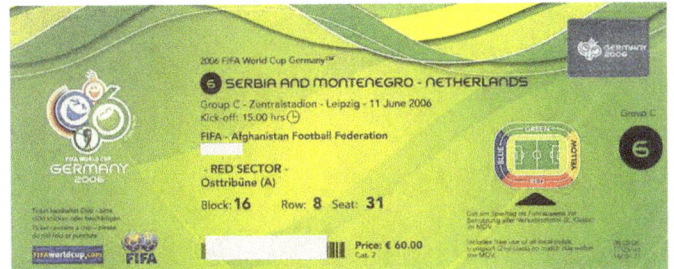

Afghanistan Football Federation! You didn't believe me did you?!

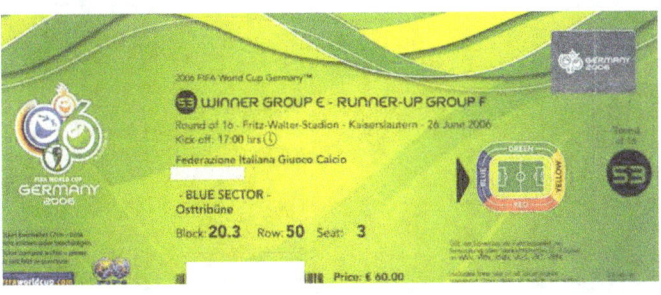

The ticket I bought on the streets of Kaiserslautern one and a half hours before the Italy vs Australia game. Again, the critical ID number is hidden. As can be seen this ticket started its life being allocated by FIFA to the Italian Federation. In this case, it is my belief that the person who sold me the ticket was a genuine Aussie fan who himself had bought a pair of tickets from the Italian who, in all probability, had been allocated the tickets legitimately by the Italian Federation in its own ticket distribution exercise.

A legitimate ticket allocated to me by the Ticket Shop of the official World Cup website. This is for a second phase match. The participating teams were unknown at the time was printed. Thus, it indicates, "Winner Match 57– Winner Match 58." This turned out to be Germany vs Italy in the semi-final. The ticket, the result of a second chance ballot, was sent to me by mail several weeks before the tournament commenced. It is personalised with my name.

Quintessentially Australian.

The all over look!

CROATIA AUSTRALIA STUTTGART 22.06.2006

Critical final game in Group F for Australia.

A bob each way!

The curtain raiser — 5-a-side in a Stuttgart square.

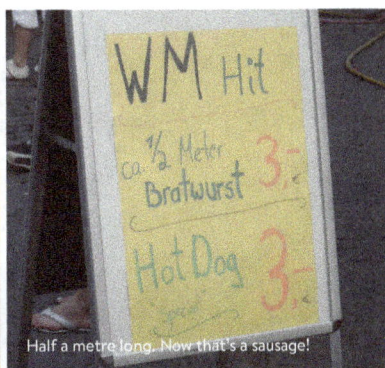
Half a metre long. Now that's a sausage!

Australia and Italy take the field in Kaiserslautern.

Australia 2 : 2 Croatia. Into the next round... Exultant!!

World Cup Maths!!! (Germany won the World Cup in 1954, 1974 and 1990) This picture was taken one hour before the Germany vs Italy semi-final. Nice idea but sadly, two and half hours later the prediction hadn't quite worked.

The spirit of the whole event. An example of the German people warming to the experience and getting involved. Near Stuttgart's Schlossplatz, the guy on the left in the wheelchair is a local and taking on all comers.

The Pinks in static mode - well, sort of
(Courtesy Josef Schmitt at www.lautringer.de)

CHAPTER TEN
AUSTRALIA IN UNCHARTED WATERS

I had been planning this World Cup ever since it was announced that Germany had won the right to stage the tournament. My close friend who lives in Berlin and with whom I stayed, was advised, "I'm coming, you know, if Germany gets the 2006 World Cup." I have probably been planning it much longer in the general sense. I have always wanted to go to a World Cup – the whole thing – but never been able to get away from work for the necessary time.

It's perverse, I know. Here I was, fully immersed in the World Cup, in the country where it was taking place, enjoying every minute of it and yet, still, I wondered from time to time, how it was being covered at home. What was I missing? What are Les "and the team" making of it. Les Murray would always sign off his nightly sports news segment on the SBS television channel, "From the team..."

SBS-TV was the channel with the broadcasting rights to the World Cup in Australia and I knew they would be doing it so well. One thing I felt I was missing was the TV replays and, of course, everything was very much centred on the German team. All of the games I had been to, I had only seen them in real time and so my memory was based on that. I know, I know... nice to able to say that... but you know what I mean. I worried a tad that I might write things in my diary about what this, that, or the other player did and yet, memory having failed me, be totally wrong. Please bear with me.

Before I left Australia I had bought Murray's recently published book, wonderfully entitled, *By the Balls*, and subtitled, *Memoirs of a Football Tragic*.

THE TIME OF MY FOOTBALL LIFE

I started reading the book on the plane over and knocked it off within a couple days. A great read and if you needed convincing, Les really is a football tragic. The book covers the flight of Les and his family from Hungary after the 1956 rebellion against the Russian controlled rulers of that nation, right through to pretty much the present. He charts his life and explains how he became, first, enchanted by football and then hopelessly and irretrievably addicted to it.

He recounts the many failures of Australian football to make it to the World Cup final stages after the one solitary appearance in Germany 1974. I have shared in two of those failures - against Iran in 1997 and against Uruguay in 2001 - so I have had just a small share of the pain as well as the unbridled joy of being in Sydney in November 2005, for the momentous victory over Uruguay.

So, we were back in Kaiserslautern again. Scene of Australia's wonderful start to the tournament. I met one of the Green and Gold Army organisers, Macca, on the train after changing at Mannheim. He has supported Australia all over the place. He had been in Europe from late May and went to the friendlies against the Netherlands and Lichtenstein. Last time we talked was in the Charles Dickens Tavern in Collins Street, Melbourne, after the pre World Cup friendly against Greece – Australia's last game at home before leaving for Europe.

At that stage I didn't even have my FFA allocated Croatia ticket. So, my talk on the train was about having gone to two of Australia's three games so far and what a night it was in Stuttgart. Boy, was the whole carriage in a buoyant mood. We were going to beat these Italians. At that stage, I thought the Fan Fest in the city would have to do.

It was obvious from the conversations though that there would be tickets available. And so it turned out to be. There were plenty of tickets on the streets and

(OR HOW I SPENT MY LONG SERVICE LEAVE)

I resolved to play a waiting game. One hour before the kick-off was my deadline. I got approached fairly early on by scalpers who were after 300 Euro for a 60 Euro ticket, but I declined. One person, a non-scalper, to my eye just a regular Aussie supporter seemed to be selling a spare ticket. Maybe one of his group had been unable to come to Germany. If you were buying in a group you had to stick with the number ordered and could be left with tickets if members failed to come up with the dosh to come over. This guy wanted 500 for an 80 ticket; that was a bit rich and I told him so. He wasn't scalping as a business enterprise, so to speak, but he was trying to scalp.

The Fan Mile area, that is the main street leading to the Fan Fest site, was wall to wall with people. Little squares had throngs of people – drinking beer, eating and singing. The one thing we have over many countries is that the world's popular songs are in the English language. When you get into this celebratory public singing we have an advantage, and so it proved here.

One small square was heaving with Aussies, they seemed to be all piled up like a little mountain on the dais of the small central feature. From somewhere Australian songs were thundering out – all the anthems, Holy Grail, Beds are Burning, Down Under. Over the previous couple of weeks I had fancied that Eagle Rock would be a goodee but it hadn't been given an airing. Maybe one for next time.

Anyway, it was all good, you could hear the raucous sound along the streets, and you were inexorably drawn in. It led me to where I was going anyway – to *Brauhaus Am Markt*, the Green and Gold Army meeting place as advised on the web site. I met with folks of a like mind and had a couple of glasses. Still ticketless, I handed over my Surf Coast FC banner to Macca who said he was off to the ground early to get a good spot for the Green and Gold Army banner.

He said he would do the best for me.

When I got in the ground eventually, I was at the opposite end and I could pick it out just above pitch level (great) and to the left of one of the goals. It would cost a fair quid for advertising there, I reckon, that's for sure! A bloke in the row in front of me had what looked like a serious camera and zoom lens and I asked him, "What can you do with that thing, mate? Can you pick up that banner at the far end?" Great job he did, giving me a preview in the little window in the camera back. I gave him my email address in the hope he would come good. Obviously the banner didn't make the telly in close up (no SMS messages from home to tell me) but with that position I decided I would be studying the DVD of the game in fine detail.

My ticket cost 250 for a 60 Euro ticket. I bought it from an Aussie lad. He seemed genuine enough when he said he had bought it from an Italian and had to buy a pair. He was only owning up to having one other ticket and they were both a tad bent (so not a scalper with style for sure). I checked when I got in there that he was sitting where he said he would be and that was correct. He wanted 300 (a price I knew other people had paid earlier in the day) but after he said he would take 270, I said, "250 and it's a deal."

The name on the ticket? I know that's what you are itching to know. *Federazione Italiana Giuoco Calcio!!!* I was a bit worried as I strolled up the stadium looking for my Blue Zone signs. The Italians would surely fill one end or more – and I felt uneasy about this.. Well, clearly the Italian Football Federation's tickets had found their way onto the market in considerable numbers. There were Aussies either side of me, in front of me, and loads of others around – I was by no means outnumbered.

I'm sure you know what happened in the game.

The Socceroos gave a good account of themselves. We had several chances

(OR HOW I SPENT MY LONG SERVICE LEAVE)

and could easily have won the game. Equally so, Italy could have won. Arguably, Australia missed an opportunity having played almost 40 minutes of the game with a one man advantage after Marco Materazzi was sent off. A harsh sending off as some would have it, but no more harsh than the dreadful refereeing decision that handed victory to Italy: Italian defender Fabio Grosso's dive fooling the referee into thinking he had been tripped by Lucas Neill. Francesco Totti converted the resulting penalty that came so late there wasn't even time to restart the game. Australia had been eliminated.

I met George Negus (journalist and TV personality from Australia and former Board member of the old Soccer Australia) after the game at Kaiserslautern, outside the railway station. It's strange, you are walking along, and you look up and there is a face that is so familiar to you – I had been watching George on the television for about 15 years or more.

He was just like he is on the telly. A nice bloke! Didn't give me the flick. I talked to him for about 15 minutes. Michael Lynch of Melbourne's Age newspaper came up. David Mitchell – ex Socceroo from the 1986 and 1990 campaigns came up. I thought that it was, perhaps, time to make my exit, but George just paused to introduce them to me, "This is Dave from Geelong!" and carried on talking; I couldn't shut the bugger up!! (I mean that in a nice way, George).

It's odd though when you meet people who are in the public eye, you know their faces and there is this automatic urge to say, for example in this case, "Hello, George," and then quickly you add, "You don't know me, but I know you." I found myself in just the same position with the other two.

Two great quotes from George. First, on the match we had just attended. "You have to remember, Dave," he said, "We were playing the biggest cheats in world football!!" Second one, was that he had been on a link back home and had suggested the Socceroos and the Australian presence in general for the World Cup in Germany, had done more for Australia's image internationally than our being in Iraq.

On the train home some people got off at Mannheim and into the spare seat beside me was Phil from Melbourne. We quickly started to chat about the game – sad at the result; should have scored a couple ourselves against ten men etcetera.

We got to talking about tickets, as you do. Bemoaning the shonky approach by FFA and so on.

Naturally enough, I told him my Afghanistan FA story. At which he looked at me and said, "I think I've got one as good, if not better." I still think Afghanistan just shades it given the nature of life there, but he said, "Do you want to see my ticket for today?" Apparently, he bought it the day before the game and paid 350 for a 60 Euro ticket. He took the ticket out of his bag and there it was – Bangladesh Football Association!! I asked him to scan it when he got home and email me a copy. Sadly, he didn't come through with that.

Round of 16

26 June 2006, Fritz Walter Stadium, Kaiserslautern

Italy   1 : 0   Australia

Totti 90+5' (pen)

Referee: Luis Medina Cantalejo (Spain)

Attendance: 46,000

CHAPTER ELEVEN
JUST A BIT DISTORTED

We in Australia are as bad as any when it comes to taking a one-eyed view of the sports news. Fair enough, the story of the Sydney Olympics was Cathy Freeman wherever you were on the planet.

However, what we were not being made aware of, and I quote these just as examples, was that Great Britain was having its best games since Antwerp in 1920 (leave aside the distorted figures of 1984, when the USSR did not participate), and Marion Jones became the first woman to win five medals in athletics at the same Olympics (forfeited later under a drug scandal we should add).

We were getting the same thing in Germany, only I think those blokes were much 'better' at it. In fact, they were veritable *Weltmeisters*, to coin a phrase. The broadsheet Berliner Morgenpost had, every day since 7th June (two days before the tournament started), been running a World Cup Supplement. The whole back page was stats, group tables, game analysis. There was a key head to head comparison of two players in opposition the previous day. I loved the depth of coverage, to tell the truth.

It was, though, the front page that interested me here. This, remember was the World Cup 2006 (WM 2006) supplement – not Germany's World Cup 2006 supplement. Take the previous Saturday's paper as an example of a day old German win upstaging a major upset result which was the hot, current news. The sequence of events going into the latter end of the week was: Germany plays quarter final on Thursday night, wins in penalty shootout; Friday morning's supplement front page photo is of German team members exultant as Jens Lehmann parried the Argentinian Roberto Ayala's spot kick to clinch the tie. Fair enough, that picture captured the story of the previous day's key game.

Then, Friday evening France eliminates Brazil. Excellent game but something of a surprise result with Brazil, among the pre-tournament favourites, going out 1-0. In addition, France had stumbled through the earlier group stages, and was in high dudgeon from four years ago going out at the group stage without scoring a goal.

Against Brazil it was Frenchman Zinedine Zidane rolling back the years and really turning on the style against the style masters themselves. Franck Ribéry, the find of the tournament in my view, caused Brazil problems all night down the right with his pace, control, and incisive running. Thierry Henry volleyed a superb goal (with a 'not as easy as it looks' aplomb) after a looping Zidane pass from a free kick. Amazingly, the record books tell us that even though these two, among the best France has ever produced, have been teammates in 60-odd internationals, Henry had never scored a goal from a 'Zizou' pass before.

And what was the front page photo in Saturday's supplement? A reworking of the photo (slightly more close up) of the German team members at their moment of victory on Thursday night. I mean, really, what was the story of the night before?

We got the same thing in the paper on 6th July. The night before France had won again – not the greatest of games but they had won through to the World Cup Final. Surely, this was the story. But no, the WM supplement front page photo was of German fans holding a banner saying thank you to their team ("The young 'uns,'" it calls them), coach Jurgen Klinsmann and Franz Beckenbauer head of the tournament organising committee. "Thanks to a cool World Cup team," it said.

(OR HOW I SPENT MY LONG SERVICE LEAVE)

Yes, fine, but what was the World Cup story on the morning of Thursday, 6th July? You had go to page 7 for that. There was but a little score block only: 'Semi-final Portugal 0 – France 1' was all it said on the front page.

Probably my favourite example of blinkers by the paper, though, was in its back page feature every day – a 'World Cup Top 10'. We had the Top 10 English penalty taking failures. Fair cop, but not sure why a goalkeeper should have featured in that though, given that it is a well-known adage in football, 'Don't blame a goalie for failing to save a penalty.'

The very idea of a penalty is punishment for a foul by the defending team (aiming to prevent a likely score) and really ought to be a certain goal. We had Top 10 players' hairstyles and there were some crackers for sure. Top 10 golf players among footballing personalities. Did you know, the then Dutch team coach Marco van Basten plays off one? Former England players, Gary Lineker and Bryan Robson came in second and third, off four and five respectively. I believe Bobby Charlton is handy in propelling the white pill too, so maybe research a bit off there, but all good fun.

Not good fun and an example of downright selective research was the Top 10 World Cup Louts listing. Basically, a rogues gallery of the World Cup's dirtiest ever players. There were some fair ones there, Horacio Troche of Uruguay in the 1966 comp (first in a long line of Uruguayans this bloke). Nobby Stiles, of England, certainly took no prisoners. The distinguished members of the academy, were there on merit, as it were, for sure. However, how on earth they could not have found a slot for their very own Harald 'Toni' Schumacher, Germany's goalkeeper in 1982, was beyond me?

This man perpetrated perhaps the worst foul in the history of the game, let alone the World Cup, when he took out French player Patrick Battiston with a calculated hip and shoulder, which smashed the Frenchman's jaw such that it required wiring together through major surgery. Battiston did not play for a year.

Just to show that selective vision for referees is not a new phenomenon, Schumacher was not even cautioned for the contact – you have to say contact as to say tackle would give it a dignity it did not deserve. If ever there was a case for post-match video inspection and retrospective punishments for player indiscretions, this was it.

In fact, I have another favourite of how the German press never lets the facts get in the way of a good story. On my second day in Germany I was looking at a photo exhibition in the entrance hall of Frankfurt station. The exhibition had been mounted by German football magazine 'Kicker.' The theme was Germany's performances in the World Cup over the years. Each competition in which Germany has played – qualified at every attempt (two being as host) it has to be said – has a single photo panel dedicated to it.

There was 1954, when Germany, having been thrashed 8–3 earlier in the tournament by the legendary Hungarian team, proceeded to manufacture a win against the same opposition in the final for what is probably the biggest upset in World Cup history. The word *Weltmeister* is emblazoned across the board. It goes on for each four yearly competitions with a definitive photograph linked to Germany's story. Then I thought to myself, oh, oh, 1966 is coming up round the corner and I knew what that photo was going to be.

In the 1966 final England played Germany (West Germany as it was then). The incident every German football fan (and a few more besides) will recount is when England scored a third goal – the game having gone into extra time at 2–2. Geoff

(OR HOW I SPENT MY LONG SERVICE LEAVE)

Hurst received the ball with his back to the goal and almost in one movement, swivelled and hammered the ball against the underside of the German crossbar. The ball came down very close to the line if not on it, but seemingly shading toward the goal side.

Years of forensic study, microscopic analysis of photographs, and the application of ballistics theory have shown that the ball was not completely over the line and, therefore, a goal should not have been given. The Azerbaijani (then Soviet Union) linesman Tofiq Bahramov was fully 30 metres away so what would he know and yet, when consulted by the Swiss referee Gottfried Dienst, he was adamant the ball was over the line, and a goal was awarded to England.

In those days, we didn't have the interminable, backwards, sideways, reverse angle replays we do now - not that it would have made any difference then - and those of us watching on TV were none the wiser.

German fans will tell you, Germany lost the World Cup to a goal that never was. What they omit to tell you was that seventeen and a half minutes later Hurst unleashed a left footer that went between German goalkeeper Hans Tilkowski's right ear and the goalpost like an Exocet missile and was - how, can I put this gently? - over the line more than just a tad.

Hurst became the first, and still, the only man to score a hat trick in a World Cup final. Seconds earlier amid scenes of players and spectators unsure as to whether the game had ended, BBC commentator Kenneth Wolstenholme, uttered the first half of his priceless epithet, "People are on the pitch... they think it's all over..." and, as Hurst's shot thundered into the net, "...it is now." It's odd that Wolstenholme years later was to say that he didn't think the last three were his actual words. Sorry Ken, I was watching the telly that day and that is exactly what you said. I have the video on DVD, and I've checked.

The third goal shouldn't have been given, it's true, but the ball certainly hit the goal line, and so as I rounded the corner to see the 1966 panel, I somehow knew that Kicker's photo archivists would have come up with something. They did not disappoint me, which is nice, I suppose.

Let's first accept their picture wasn't doctored; it's just that it had been selected from those that were taken a second (maybe less) either before or after the ball struck the ground. Thus, with the foreshortening effect the ball looks to be well in the field of play. Blinkers?!! You would need very funny eyes and a puff of wacky backy to believe that photo gave anything like a true reflection of the incident.

CHAPTER TWELVE

PLAYED AGAINST SOMEONE INVOLVED IN THE WORLD CUP!!

One day I found my connection to the World Cup as a football player! Excuse me?!! Come on, Dave, this is going a bit too far! Bear with me, it is not one of those, 'I know a bloke whose cousin's friend's sister once swept the floor after..." – well, not really, honest. I was browsing the FIFA World Cup web site and amongst the official FIFA staff I found the name of a guy that I once played against.

What I was actually looking for was some serious analysis of the refereeing in this tournament. I know, it was like looking for rocking horse doo-doo, though you can but try. The most damning comment I've read was after two weeks of the programme, when Sepp Blatter, FIFA's Secretary General, in giving a sort of half-term report, suggested the quality of refereeing had not been as good as the standard of play thus far.

This was even before Russian referee, Valentin Ivanov, became the first referee in history to look to the fourth official for a replacement yellow card. His first one had become sweaty and crumpled by being removed from his pocket so often. (He didn't really ask for a new card, I just made that up!)

Ivanov did, however, issue 20 yellow cards in one match. You could say 16 yellow and four red cards. Depends on how you count them actually – he issued 16 and four players received second yellow cards and these four players then, according to the rules, were shown a red card – expelled from the field. That is, for a player who receives two yellow cards in the one game, it's time to break out the body scrub and sing in the shower by yourself. Except in this case, by the time Mr Ivanov had completed his night's work they had a barber shop quartet in there.

I do get myself in a real tizz with referees, and umpires in other sports, who proceed to have an influence on the outcome of games for which it should not be their prerogative. Being taken in by play acting in some cases, in others not so much taken in, but actually believing there was unfair contact when a player has merely tumbled over due to the sheer physical, but fair, presence of the opposition player.

Awarding penalty kicks that are dubious, at best, at critical moments of a game, when to adjudge that a contact was 50/50 and to allow play to continue is only fair to the defending team. For the defending team to get the better of the decision, gives them a clearing free kick. For the attacking team, it is a clear shot on goal from the penalty spot. Slightly out of kilter in terms of the potential outcome. Very often in these cases a quick, firm decision by the ref not to award a penalty would produce no quibble by the attacking team.

In all of this, though, I am still not completely sure about the introduction of replay technology. I still believe in the idea that football is about human frailties as much as it is about skill. What I would advocate is to introduce the after match video review and to punish players who are shown to be play acting, 'simulating' the rule book calls it, to deceive the referee.

This would go for diving when little, or no, contact is made and also that other little bit of Oscar-seeking work – screaming in agony (you can hear them on the telly sometimes) and clutching a part of the anatomy that was nowhere near the point at which they came into contact with the opposing player.

(OR HOW I SPENT MY LONG SERVICE LEAVE)

For example, clutching the left shin when right leg was contacted. Or, after a mere brush of the neck by a trailing hand, grasping the whole face as if major plastic surgery will be required before their sponsor will even consider putting them in a product promotion TV shoot again.

I digress. What about my World Cup playing connection? I knew that FIFA has a so-called Technical Studies Group (TSG) at the World Cup (in fact, has had them since the 1966 World Cup). 1966, eh? So that's the reason England has failed to even reach the final since then – too much technical study helping the other countries.

Seriously, the group monitors all games and comments on playing standards and tactical approaches. The group comprises 14 people, either ex-players or ex-coaches (sometimes they are both) at international level. Two group members are assigned to each game and one produces a report which you can read on the web site. The list of members names people such as Teófilo Cubillas (a great Peruvian player), likewise Roger Milla of Cameroon. Jozef Vengloš of Slovakia, a world renowned coach, who is known to the football community in Australia. Jim Selby, who was head of football coaching development at Football Federation Australia was a member of the group.

I was checking out the reports to see if they got stuck into the referees at all. Well, I can tell you now that they did not. I wondered if, perhaps, it was not in the brief, I thought, and it transpired that, indeed, it was not. Based on the web site reports it seemed like a pretty easy job. None of the reports were more than 300 words or so and most were somewhat platitudinous.

I know plenty of amateurs producing match reports for online forums that could do the same. When I dug a little deeper I found that more in-depth reports would be prepared, DVDs would be made and disseminated to FIFA's member associations around the world for development and coaching. So, there was quite a deal of work for the TSG to do when the tournament was over.

Listed among the TSG members I found, to my surprise, Mr Kwok Ka-Ming of Hong Kong. I immediately recognised his name. He played for Hong Kong's national team in the 1970s and participated in World Cup qualifying tournaments.

Hong Kong, because of its lowly ranking, had to go through a number of qualifying levels before it even got to the Asian Football Confederation's qualifiers proper, but it was the World Cup, whichever way you cut it. I recall on one famous occasion they turned over the People's Republic of China side in Beijing in a World Cup qualifier. A great occasion for Hong Kong. Like Australia beating England at West Ham's ground in 2003.

I lived in Hong Kong between 1979 and 1995 and I guess you could say it was a bit of a swan song for me as a football player. In our league (so called Yau Yee – that is, Friendly – League), there was a team called Fortress Hill who seemed to have connections with the Hong Kong FA.

I believe it was a couple of the lads on the admin staff at the HKFA that organised a side. It was a 'Friendly' League, though not meaning ad hoc matches. There was a full home and away programme, but we didn't really bother about ringers or non-registered players – life is too short. From time to time, if Fortress Hill were a bit light on for players they might ask some of the HKFA coaching staff and maybe even a couple of likely youngsters from the development squads to turn out for them. And this is where my connection arose.

On a couple occasions against our university staff team they had Kwok Ka-Ming in their side – basically to run the show from midfield, and when he felt

(OR HOW I SPENT MY LONG SERVICE LEAVE)

like it, or so they thought, he can just turn it on, pop in a couple; three points, thank you very much, see you later.

I played against Kwok a few times. He was a HKFA coach and well past his prime but then so was I at the age of 35. Some of our lads who knew his pedigree got the jitters when he showed up, but for my part I resolved to enjoy it. I made sure I was his shadow, but also tried to do some creative things myself. We never lost to Fortress Hill and Kwok never scored. At the end he made a special point to shake my hand and say, "Well played." That was good enough for me.

So, who monitored the referees? The short answer is – I haven't got a clue. On the web site the word 'Referees' was clickable but all it produced was a list of names, the only further links gave the refereeing CV of each person listed. There was assessment of the referees and culling of the list as the tournament moved into the later stages. Graham Poll was one who got the tap on the shoulder and was handed the plane ticket home after the group stages.

Obviously that sort of decision was not an informal back of an envelope type of thing, but the inner workings of the refereeing committee was buried deeper than the whereabouts of a secret service safe house.

CHAPTER THIRTEEN
DORTMUND: SEMI-FINAL DAY

I was on the train from Berlin to Dortmund. It was World Cup semi-final day. My ticket, rather coldly I felt, merely said, (match number) 61. Winner match 57 – Winner Match 58, semi-final Kick off 21:00.

What that had turned out to be, in fact, was Germany vs Italy. Both teams are former three time winners of the competition. The following night would be Portugal and France going round in Munich in the other semi.

This game was the last one I would attend at the World Cup. I was really quite excited. A World Cup semi-final? In terms of sheer status in the game, this was the most important match I had been to. I have been to a few FA Cup finals at the old Wembley, but this was the top for me.

It was almost inconceivable that the game would not be a spectacle. There would, I was sure, be drama, tension, heartache for the losers and joy unconfined for the winners who would go on to the final in Berlin.

The German team had got the country's collective steam engine of enthusiasm, as it were, going full bore and the pressure meter needle was inching towards the red zone. It really was a step by step tightening of the valve.

They opened up with goals (four to be precise) against Cost Rica. Not one of the world's footballing powers but, as they say, the ball has to be stuck in the net no matter who the opposition is. Then they snatched victory in the dying seconds against Poland – a win which, if it didn't light the fuse, certainly had

(OR HOW I SPENT MY LONG SERVICE LEAVE)

the matchstick poised over the touch paper. Subsequently, they had progressed from the quarters to the semi-final on the strength of a penalty shootout against Argentina. They did that comfortably – none of their designated penalty takers missed and their goalie saved two of Argentina's attempts – but the shootout always sets the pulse racing.

I knew that if Germany won the game there would be pandemonium. But what if they lost? Who knows? If it was a win, the song their fans had been singing for the past three weeks now (oddly enough, given their semi-final opponents, to the tune of the old Italian hit *Volare*) – "Finale, oh, oh" – would no longer be a prediction it would be a reality.

Their opponents, Italy, we cannot mention without an "Australia – what might have been?" ballad. It doesn't achieve anything at all I know but I'll engage in it anyway, I don't care. Australia could so easily have beaten Italy (could have lost too, if Italy had slotted their own chances earlier in the game). I will not claim that Australia would have won in extra time, but they would have given it a damn good shake. Instead, Italy went through courtesy of a very dubious penalty awarded in the final seconds. No time to even restart after Totti had whipped it home.

Italy breezed past Ukraine in the quarter final and I suspect Australia would have done the same. Certainly nothing to fear from Ukraine as long as you kept Andriy Shevchenko under close supervision. Australia in the semi-final was by no means the pie in the sky that was suggested. Certainly not in terms of the team and its capabilities. Sadly, the public here and the rest of the world outside of Australia think it was a flash in the pan. With justification, perhaps, based on the bare facts with this being only the second appearance in the finals for 32 years and, with no disrespect to the team, in 1974, we were a novelty side.

Anyway, Germany vs Italy. I was going for Germany. Not to do so would be disrespectful to Ingrid, my dear friend and host in Berlin.

I couldn't get my head around Italy despite my Italian heritage. Lots of people will say I look Italian. I believe there is a distant connection on the maternal side, but I'm afraid I did not inherit what we might call their 'football perspective' gene. The Italian players are the classic, scream out when tackled slightly harder than a slap with wet lettuce; roll over three times when once would be excessive; shrugged shoulders combined with upturned palms that would win gold medals in the, "Who me, ref?" competition.

The softee when tackled, 'Owwwh, you've messed my hair up now,' style is intriguing when you look back over the years at the hard men of Italian football. I'll recall just one gentleman who rejoiced in the moniker of Antonello Cuccureddu – it sounds like a hard player's name doesn't it? They had another one just the same in Germany, Gennaro Gattuso, which is a name that sounds like he would take you off at the neck – he went in hard for sure but made like a nancy boy when he copped one himself. Conversely, the name Roberto Baggio does not sound hard, it sounds artistic and he was.

The story I remember about Cuccureddu is one reputedly from the England team at the time. Two team members were discussing the Italian players. One mentioned the Cucc's name and when the other guy looked quizzical, he said, "Oh, you know, the guy who looks like he shaves with a blowtorch!!"

While I was daydreaming, recalling these Italian players, the train was tootling along at 230kph according to the read out on the digital board in our carriage. I say, tootling, because it really is that kind of sensation where you think,

(OR HOW I SPENT MY LONG SERVICE LEAVE)

"It doesn't feel that fast at all." The countryside wasn't a blur; and the train wasn't rocking and rolling. I suppose it must become a blur of sorts when you get up to the 300s – I don't know – but this was great.

The Italian team, though. Take away the acting performances of Oscar-winning calibre, they are bloody good at the World Cup caper. Usually a very good keeper and sometimes downright brilliant, and the bloke Gianluigi Buffon was in the latter category and I suspected he was a shoo-in for the 'Best in Show' XI which FIFA will nominate. Brilliantly marshalled defences with players in charge like Fabio Cannavaro (in Germany) and Franco Baresi and Paolo Maldini (formerly). Cunning, wily, and yet skilful midfielders (Andrea Pirlo, Gianluca Zambrotta and the aforementioned Gattuso) who could cruelly expose teams, and strikers who finish clinically. Maybe we will see this Italy tonight. If Germany are on too, the game would be cracker.

In my pondering I supposed if there was a god of irony, tonight's result would be a 1-0 win to Germany through a last minute dodgy penalty decision. The crowd would go wild at Germany's victory and we could engage in singing to the Italians, "How does it feel? How does it f-ee – e-l?" To the tune of Bob Dylan's "Like a Rolling Stone." Well, I would sing it in my mind, at any rate.

The poetic justice result rarely happens, though, so I'd just be satisfied with end to end stuff, some great skill on show, 2-2 draw after 90 minutes and settled by proper football in extra time. No penalty shoot-out – don't like them. Or, I only like them if players like Portugal's Ronaldo miss – then you can heap upon them the unadulterated scorn that they deserve or sing, "You can't always get what you want!!"

Semi-Finals

4 July 2006, FIFA World Cup Stadium (Signal Iduna Park), Dortmund

Germany   0 : 2   Italy (aet)

                    Grosso 119'

                    Del Piero 120'

Referee: Benito Archundia (Mexico)

Attendance: 65,000

CHAPTER FOURTEEN
THERE'S BUSKERS AND THEN THERE'S BUSKERS

For our purposes here, buskers refers to anyone who engages in street performance of music or other skill displayed in public and in some cases, though not always, part of the equipment may be a tin or hat in which to collect money from appreciative passers-by.

I saw all sorts in Germany – some were fairly orthodox in today's terms. There was your basic street musician, though none I found stunning. Sometimes the musicians perform in the train strolling down the carriage, hopping from one carriage to another at successive stops. These buskers I found oppressive as they were forcing their performance upon me and I was disinclined to contribute to the cause.

One innovation I saw was a number of street musicians with a small, puppet-like model of themselves - same clothes, same instrument, and the puppet mimicked their playing, courtesy of a string attached to the musician's tapping foot.

There were a number of those folks who did the statue thing. Typically dressed and made up from head to toe to give a metallic or stone look. They struck a pose and proceed to hold, dead still, for minutes on end. Many stood on a pedestal giving their trick an increased tariff, to use a term to define aquatic diving difficulty. There were some very good ones, but I have seen better elsewhere in the world. Oddly, none used the World Cup theme. No Pelé statues, for example.

My first special one was a juggler – he was dressed in a Brazil shirt and certainly had a Latin look to his face, so I am assuming he was indeed, Brazilian. This man had a disability, seemingly unable to walk without the aid of crutches. His legs had the disposition of one who has suffered from polio and his baggy jeans perhaps hid the definitive leg callipers. He had turned to his disability to develop his particular trick. He juggled a football with his elbow length crutches. He was incredible. His juggling sessions went on for minutes on end. The crutches flicked up the ball, then encircled it as it was in mid-air. The knocks and nudges on the ball employed the full length of the crutch stems; back and forth the ball travelled. Up and down, little bop, bop dibbles; bigger looping arcs, and even on to the rubber tips of the crutches.

Just when you thought there might be a trick of sorts, a weighted ball maybe, he would knock the ball upwards and on to his head and bobbed it up and down with headers. Up and down several times Ronaldinho style. This fella cannot run up and down a football field of course, but I wonder if the Brazilian players (typically prodigious ball jugglers) could handle the crutches as well as this bloke?

Bob, bob, bob the ball went off his forehead and then just a touch higher and his head rocked forward so he could catch the ball on the back of his neck. No problem with this – he held it in the nape quite easily and then, to restart the routine, flicked his head upwards with a jerk. Up went the ball and down on to his crutches again. A mesmerising performance you were compelled to watch.

There were pavement artists who were extremely talented briefly immortalising World Cup players in coloured chalks. I saw one guy whose talent was chess playing. He would take on all comers, two at a time when I was watching but he

(OR HOW I SPENT MY LONG SERVICE LEAVE)

had other boards and boxes, other chess sets I assumed, so I'm unsure on how many he was prepared to take on simultaneously. Oddities were the saxophone player with a parrot on his head - honestly. Certainly a strange combination. His sax playing was goodish, but I didn't work out the subtlety of the parrot's role. Sharing the story with others, they recounted seeing the same bloke and that sometimes he kissed the parrot, which seemed to return his affection – still not convinced though.

In Stuttgart a short time after Australia's game against Croatia, we saw a guy in the *Schlossplatz* who did various acrobatic tricks whilst bouncing up and down on a pogo stick. This was a serious piece of equipment, not your 1960s toy with bike tubing and a heavy duty spring, but more like an oversized jackhammer with footrests. His final trick was to jump the pogo stick over two audience volunteers. They were lying side by side, not head to toe, so it didn't appear to be too difficult as he was getting prodigious vertical jumps out of this thing in his normal routine. Clearly, though, it is difficult to jump the pogo a long way horizontally. He took three attempts, the first two aborted, possibly for a dramatic effect, but on the last one, with a heaving jerk he came up off the rebound and cleared the prostrate volunteers (Australian and proud of it) and came down with a crash but ensured he fell away from them.

The best ones were in Kaiserslautern, which had very different acts. The first I saw comprised of four characters who wore costume structures to make them about three metres tall. The outward look was of a cartoon-like head, big nose, no neck, and topped off with a black bowler hat about four sizes too small. They wore brown, ankle-length raincoats.

The overall effect to my eyes was almost Kafkaesque – they stared at people and nodded knowingly at one another, the heads being operated like puppets from below. If an onlooker took too long to stare at them or over taking a photo, they bent at the waist (the waist of the three metre figure) and went nose to nose as if to say, "Who are you staring at?"

They would work in pairs and then come back together as a four, where they stood in line looking left and right superciliously and completed the session with looks exchanged as if to say, dismissively, "What odd people these are! We are wasting our time here." And off they would go to harass other people. There was much joviality among the onlookers, and it seemed as if the four had brought to life well-known TV cartoon characters which I had not heard of.

My favourite of all, though, was a group which I called 'The Pinks.' These seven men were in the, how shall I say, 'old enough to know better' category. Their angle was playing guitar instrumentals. In particular, they played Shadows music from the 1960s.

The former backing group of Cliff Richard had a purple patch back then, when their Fender electric guitar music was very popular – Apache, Wonderful Land, FBI – the list goes on. The Pinks went through the card. They were buskers; they played in the street, yes, but there was more than that. The musicianship was great, and they attracted quite a crowd in Kaiserslautern's Fan Mile. In fact, the street was packed so there was always going to be a crowd, but they were a mobile band and it was the manner of the moving that was intriguing. They were playing music, remember, that needs to be amplified.

The set up was six guitarists standing side by side in pairs, each bloke had his own amplifier on a little bogey-like trolley and the bogeys were linked, as if into a kiddie's push along train. They would be stationary for several minutes and

(OR HOW I SPENT MY LONG SERVICE LEAVE)

play a few numbers and then, on the signal of the leader (the guy in the Hank Marvin role we might say), they would move to a new spot. Each amp trolley had an upholstered bar coming up off the frame and into a U-shaped rail at about waist height.

On the signal from 'Hank', he and the other guys, still continuing to play, would gently slide, almost jiggle their way, into the U and slowly, slowly move their little train along with a countenance of, 'Look, mum, no hands!'

At the back, and centrally placed, the seventh guy was in charge of a bigger trolley. The PA and the drum machine were housed there, along with several car batteries. As the train moved along he bopped to the music as he gently steered the whole contraption like a tillerman.

Oh sorry, I almost forgot. Why did I call them The Pinks? Well, these guys had the slicked hair thing happening and wore navy blue shirts and tailored suits of raw silk in a striking shade of cerise pink! Pink ties in the same material!! Just picture it – the warbling, sometimes jangling sounds of the Shadows as they bobbed away with their push along train and a riot of colour.

CHAPTER FIFTEEN
AUSTRALIAN PRODUCT (*SIC*)

Can someone tell me when the word 'product' came to mean both plural and singular? I must have been absent from school on that day.

These days you read newspapers and hear on the TV and radio comments such as, "It is important that we increase our stock of product to meet consumer demand." This comment could come from a supermarket representative and I would have thought that, surely, they are going to add more than one item to the shelves. Maybe? It is not sheep we are talking about – I have one sheep; I have two sheep. I have one product; I have two products. It's easy, see, just talk it through and see how daft you sound. Two sheeps? Two product? Really!

My linguist friends tell me, "Dave, relax, it's a living language." It is, I agree. Did you know that a long time ago the word for newt used to be ewt? So, people in those days would say, "He's as pissed as an ewt." Well, maybe they didn't, but it sounds colourful enough for my purposes.

What happened, linguistically, over a period of time is that the 'n' in 'an' sort of slid across towards the 'e' in 'ewt,' until it actually got stuck there making the new word newt. The same thing happened with umpire, but in reverse. Historically, they were called numpires. Doesn't it sound deliciously onomatopoeic? The sound of the word numpire has the timbre of someone who is not the quite the full quid? So, 'a numpire' became 'an umpire' as the n travelled in the opposite direction.

Hang on to your hats. Folks like me, in the 'fair play for the apostrophe' club, be prepared for the word "couldof" to enter the Concise Oxford anytime soon.

(OR HOW I SPENT MY LONG SERVICE LEAVE)

Maybe 'hone' will, by sheer weight of misuse, come to mean 'home,' although for now their meanings are totally unrelated. Don't even talk to me about agreeance, and I've given up on orient and orientate – noun, verb; who gives a rats?

I digress. The issue under scrutiny was the lack of products in shops in Germany such that you wondered whether Australia did, in fact, take part in this World Cup. I have mentioned before how you could sell the most obtuse things in Germany in Brazil colours or with a Brazil federation logo on it. You still could at the end of the tournament, even though they went out at the quarter final stage. Only a cog better than Australia and at the same hurdle as England. I have also mentioned before how I took issue (in good humour) with the young fella serving in the KaDeWe sports shop about the shortage of Australian football kit on their shelves – but trying to find an Australian replica jersey in a variety of sizes was very difficult.

My daughter needed a jersey in the small size and the day we were looking there were just oddments. A couple of XXLs and three XLs. Nike had seven other teams in tow, and you could find any amount of their stuff, even Korea Republic and Mexico. Supporters of the USA, that well-known powerhouse of world football – not – were well catered for.

In one sense, the sports goods suppliers had done their sums, as there were loads of Mexico supporters in Germany and from the conversations I had and overheard, many were over there from home and not residents of Europe. I can tell you that Nike Town Berlin had racks full of everything on 10th July (the day after the final) – that is, everything but Australia. The one set of Australia kit was on the mannequin on display.

It wasn't just the jerseys of the other nations, there were also the accessories:

tee shirts, headbands, caps, and the like. I rather fancied Australia's away jersey myself – midnight blue with an understated gold trim. The yellow jersey is for making an exhibition of yourself at games; the blue one, you could wear to work on casual dress days without jarring anyone's senses. For Nike's other countries you could often find the full set; shirt, shorts, and socks – commonly the away jersey was also available. Asking for an Australia away jersey you risked scorn and guffaws of laughter from the store's PA: "Aisle 3 – enquiring after Australia away jersey – ho, ho, ho – you've got to be joking!!"

I found my daughter's small size jersey in the unlikeliest of places. Not in Nike Town (their *Joga Bonito* promotion only having Australia as a bit part player) or any of the major stores. One of Berlin's Bundesliga sides, Hertha, has a club shop in the centre of the city. I didn't know that they were a Nike clad side but walking past their shop one day I noticed they were jumping on the Brazil bandwagon with a couple shirts displayed in the shop window. I popped in just on a whim. Maybe they have other teams and sure enough they had an Australia jersey in small – no rhyme or reason is there?

I eventually did find my away jersey but only after we dumped Croatia out of the comp by drawing with them in our final group game.

Things improved a little after that. We were taken a little more seriously. Of course, as you would expect they were caught short – the wholesale suppliers didn't have enough Australian product – for a day or two up to and including the Round of 16 game with Italy.

Wandering around Kaiserslautern's Fan Mile on the day of that game I came across a shop with a rapidly reducing stack of yellow tee shirts on which "Socceroos 2006" had been hastily printed. Selling at 8 Euro a pop and, peering

(OR HOW I SPENT MY LONG SERVICE LEAVE)

inside the shop, I could see they could not print them fast enough. Italian supporters were clearly more numerous, but the streets were heaving with Australians too, all ready and willing to buy a souvenir of some sort. The shop owner told me there was just nothing to be had from the wholesalers. Knowing that the Australians were returning to Kaiserslautern, they were desperate to have something to sell and the best was buying a job lot of yellow tee shirts and doing the printing themselves.

You never saw what we might call the accessories in the shops. No green and gold headbands, no caps. Many shops sold flags of all the nations, but Australia's was a rarity. My Berlin hosts were desperate to support me by fixing up one of those flags on a car window-clip thingees, but an Australian flag could not be found in Berlin.

I went back to KaDeWe and had a bit of sport about their football kit display. They had what was like a guard of honour of larger than life mannequins (the XXL sizes, I guess). There were eight models in two lines of four. Eight countries wearing Nike kit, but Australia was not represented in the display. Where was our mannequin in the guard of honour was what I wanted to know?

They had two Brazil-clad models, one at the head of each line, followed by three other models of the remaining six. When I asked the guy why Australia didn't feature in the parade. "Come on, mate, this is a bit rich!" Taking me quite seriously, he said, "I'm very sorry. It is not my decision, and actually one reason is that we don't have the Australian shorts!" Very thoughtful, I reckoned, of the KaDeWe shop display squad to protect Australian modesty and go for two Brazil kits to lead the lines.

The Adidas shop was packed on 10th July, the day after the final. There were queues at the checkout snaking around the store. People buying up 'product' (though more than one for sure!) like crazy. They even had for sale a tee shirt for the next World Cup, South Africa 2010, with the just released logo – jeez, these people are like the proverbial rat up a drain pipe, aren't they?

There were thirty-two boot models in the Adidas F1 range with a version for each of the participating nations. In the thirty-two boot display in the window there was one Australia boot and that's your lot. If you went inside to buy a pair there were plenty of Ivory Coast (wash my mouth out, I mean Côte D'Ivoire), which came in somewhat jarring shades of orange and green, and Tunisia boots and everyone else except Angola and Australia. The boots in the window were left boots arranged on a display board, so I don't know if they claim to even have a pair of the damn things. No disrespect to Angola but there are a few hundred Australians playing in overseas leagues and quite a number of those in Germany.

The argument of the store buyer I guess was that, "Well, you have got to be sure of getting rid of your product." Yeah, mate, you get the grammar right and I'll give you a hearing!! Surely, though, I would have thought there was a strong element of novelty buying – it certainly looked that way to me. Some of it wasn't novelty as such because it went something like, 'I'll buy one of my own and a Brazil one.' However, if folks are into buying one of their own plus a novelty one then the Australian stuff should have been on the shelf. Then it would come into play for the novelty purchase market. If it ain't on the shelf I can guarantee you one thing – nobody is going to buy it.

The one thing that really shouted at me in the Adidas store is that although Brazil was not, as they say on TV, dressed by Adidas, they still had items in the distinctive yellow and green colours, they just didn't include the word Brazil.

(OR HOW I SPENT MY LONG SERVICE LEAVE)

They have a Brazil boot in the F1 range, and they have a Brazil ball – plenty of each in stock. Like everyone else they were desperate to cash in on the anything Brazil craze.

CHAPTER SIXTEEN

THE FINAL

I watched the final at the Waldbühne, next door to the Olympic Stadium where the game actually took place. The best analogy I can give you is that it was like having a Sidney Myer Music Bowl (Melbourne's outdoor concert venue) with knobs on right alongside the Melbourne Cricket Ground and a huge video screen on the stage. Placing Hyde Park in London next door to Wembley Stadium would give the same effect.

A couple of nights before the final, as part of the more formal cultural side of the World Cup festivities, Placido Domingo and friends packed the place (I nearly said, 'to the rafters' but it's open air – you know what I mean). Not sure whether they have had any other games shown there, but for the final, despite the attractions of Berlin's *Fan Miele*, it seemed the *Waldbühne* was the big ticket if you couldn't get into the stadium. Thirty Euro just to watch the telly. I was in the fortunate position of having tickets gifted to me by friends. It was very generous of them. Understandably, had Germany made the final, I would not have been so fortunate. No doubt then the event would have been quite something – possibly outdoing the Domingo show.

Note I used the term *Fan Miele*. The Fan Fest in Berlin really was 'a mile,' rather than a focused gathering, the whole affair spread down the *Strasse des 17 Juni* from Brandenburg Gate almost to *Tiergarten*. I told you about the 50-odd thousand they were attracting early on. With Germany's continued presence in the tournament, these attendances were swelling, between 700,000 and

(OR HOW I SPENT MY LONG SERVICE LEAVE)

750,000 and around a million on a couple occasions.

It would be unfair to call the final a damp squib because it wasn't. Even so, it did fizzle and pop without really igniting (sorry, I know, that sounds like a damp squib). There was, though, much to admire.

The old men of France – six players over the age of 32 – did drag one last performance out of their legs as we had all hoped, and the game was given a real shake as an occasion by a goal scored from an outrageous penalty kick by French hero Zinedine Zidane.

It started with what, in my view, was a somewhat dodgy refereeing decision. Horacio Elizondo, he of the petulant sending off of Wayne Rooney, who was handed the honour to whistle the final. I don't mean Rooney was being petulant; I mean Elizondo, allowing himself to be sucked in by Portugal's Ronaldo.

Watch the replay. Elizondo is quite calm, at worst he is going to book Rooney for the tangle of legs with Carvalho. Rooney's is the slightest of pushes on Ronaldo, a sort of, "Nick off, what's it got to do with you?" push. It is not violent, but it certainly fires up Elizondo. For me the incredulity on the face of England player Ashley Cole told a story.

In the 7th minute of the final Elizondo fell to a sort of double deception by the Italians. What I mean is this, whilst the Italians could give Greg Louganis or Jacques Cousteau lessons in the plunging caper (choose your own diving analogy), their defenders have also developed the art of sucking attacking players into diving which, if the referee spots the play acting tumble, could result in a yellow card to the attacker.

The defender's trick is to go steaming in as if they are going to clatter the on-rushing forward and, at the last second, take away the tackling foot and leg that bears a passing resemblance to a scythe. The forward has already had the idea, 'If this bloke touches me I'm going to drop like a lead balloon.' It all happens too quickly, though, and the commitment to dive often cannot be rescinded.

The slow motion replay showed that Marco Materazzi did precisely this to Florent Malouda, but did it just too well, and the referee thought he had taken down the Frenchman. In any event, up stepped Zidane off his familiar one step run. His penalty kick style was to take just one step and employ a lashing motion of the leg, to rip the ball past the keeper low and hard. The short run gave the keeper no chance to discern a direction based on the kicker's run up. Just like the rest of us, the Italian goalie, Buffon, one of the best going round, had seen Zidane do it against Portugal in the semi-final.

Buffon's idea was to try and steal the minutest amount of time, maybe also steal a bit of space by coming off his line (against the rules but few referees spot it), and hope Zidane went to his (Buffon's) right. There was nothing in Zidane's facial expression at all, other than a steely resolve to put France one goal up. I daresay the whole world watching on television thought he was going for the lasher. Up he stepped and at the very last instant he checked his leg movement and, instead, his foot jabbed, not lashed, at the ball. Buffon, was already down to his right and looked up, aghast, as the ball gently lobbed in a delicious arc up high to his left.

The crowd, the world, went wild – some of us murmured, "You cheeky sod!!" The ball actually struck the crossbar and for a moment we thought we might have to exhume Tofik Bachramov, to adjudge whether it had gone over the line. But, no, we now had the action replay. Not used officially (though see later in this story), and for us watching on telly we quickly saw the ball was way over the line, and

(OR HOW I SPENT MY LONG SERVICE LEAVE)

vicious back spin, first imparted by Zidane's jabbing kick and then with interest added by the crossbar made it come back into the field of play. Elizondo, for his part, was immediately thrusting his arm aloft and pointing towards the centre circle – meaning, "Goal to France. Italy to restart."

So quick and firm was he, it was as if he had the Superman glasses on and had seen in real time what we had seen in replay. I'm not convinced by his demonstrative rightness, but his decision was correct. You see, I don't much care for self-righteousness in anybody, least of all referees. Self-righteousness means they always think they are right, and Elizondo will go out and referee the same way again. Will he look at the wrongness of the original penalty decision? Say it ain't so, Horacio!

Trouble is we analyse players' faults and indiscretions and sometimes allow journalists into the hearing. When will referees receive the same scrutiny?

How do you allocate the refereeing duties for a World Cup final? Simple answer is that I don't know. There is the basic requirement of the officials being independent. Elizondo is from Argentina and so fitted that bill well. There is also a fourth official (in addition to the referee and two assistants – what we used to call linesmen in the old days; or if you will, linespersons).

The fourth official would become the referee if the first bloke falls over, becomes indisposed, whatever. Who was the fourth official for the final? Luis Medina Cantalejo of Spain. This was the gentleman who officiated in Australia's Round of 16 game against Italy.

The man who thought Lucas Neill fouled Italy's Grosso only seconds before the end of the game. Remember this means he did not think it was 50/50. He thought Neill had definitely fouled Grosso. The replay, at best, suggests there was plenty of room for doubt but Cantalejo showed not a jot.

Therefore, FIFA rewarded them with plum jobs, the plum jobs; two referees who made a couple of the tournament's most dodgy refereeing decisions. We couldn't accuse the two of them of Poll-itis, I agree, but why did Australian referee Mark Shields only get the 'pat on the head, have a sugar lump, when you are a bit older son' fourth official slot in the third and fourth place play off?

Actually, Elizondo became the first referee to officiate in the opening game and the final at the one tournament.

After Australia's loss to Italy I sent an SMS message to my wife, Nicola, which went like this: *Totally undeserved. If that referee gets the final, and I fear he might, I will be doubly sick.* I could see it coming, FIFA somehow seem to like the cut of referees like Cantalejo. I could imagine Spain failing to make the final thus qualifying him on the impartiality requirement. Jigger me, he almost made it in getting the fourth official nomination.

I'll finish on referees here with a question I have had forming in my mind for some time and it is this. Question to any referee who has either got on to the FIFA list or has aspirations to do so: Given a free choice, what would you prefer; your country reaches the World Cup final or, they do not thus giving you a shot at refereeing the final? It's a bloody tricky one, isn't it? Maybe I am being unkind, but my worry is that all too many referees would answer it all too quickly and go for the second option.

Italy's overt memorable moments were the equalising goal – a comprehensive header by Materazzi from a looping Andrea Pirlo corner which bulleted past Fabien Barthez – and, a short time later, a badly defended corner by the French again resulted in another header from Luca Toni crashing against the crossbar.

(OR HOW I SPENT MY LONG SERVICE LEAVE)

The French defence looked very uncomfortable at set pieces. True, the Italians had towering presences in Materazzi and Toni to contest the artistically flighted crosses of Pirlo but then the French were not short on height in the defence. It was Patrick Vieira, no Tom Thumb, who was simply outjumped by Materazzi for the goal. Here was the Italian genius one felt, as Italian coach Marcello Lippi had clearly seen the possibilities of this line of attack. Yet again Lippi's plans were resolutely carried out with a superbly marshalled defence by Fabio Cannavaro who, in his spare time, kept Thierry Henry under close scrutiny. Strong work from Gianluca Zambrotta and Gennaro Gattuso, provided the steel threads in the midfield.

Lippi is a master tactician. The Italian squad of players was sound. There were a few class players – Buffon in goal, and Cannavaro in defence, are world class. Pirlo in midfield and Toni in attack are very good. Beyond these, Lippi welded a so-so squad into a team that improved as it progressed through the tournament. He gave them a focus by identifying a clear idea of each player's role in the overall shape of the team and demanded a steeliness that required them to concentrate on this. This focus had the double benefit of diverting their attention from a very serious scandal in football administration back home which might have severely disrupted the team.

One specific area where one could say Lippi outcoached his opposite numbers is in the use of his older players. Alessandro Del Piero and, to a lesser extent, Francesco Totti were no longer 90 minute players at international level. Lippi used Del Piero as an impact player coming on as a fairly late substitute (and he did this to great effect in the semi-final and the final). Totti was nursed through the earlier games by not being required to play a full match. Raymond Domenech, in contrast, often required his veterans to play full matches.

France dominated the final for long periods of the second half and extra time. For me, the wheels really started to fall off when Patrick Viera, the sort of player not just with the style and skill but also the resolve to match the Italians, had to pull out with a thigh strain. He was caught in slow motion clutching the back of his leg like a foot race sprinter who looks as if he's been shot at the 70 metre mark.

You didn't think it at the time but Viera had become important to the French cause, and I would aver that Domenech would have been looking to have him on the field at the end. In the final, Zidane was not in his most emphatic of moods. So complete was his performance against Brazil in the quarter final, a game which for him was arguably the zenith of his career in terms of his performance level, it was perhaps difficult to reach those heights so soon again.

Zidane was, though, pulling the strings and was the prompter behind France's attacking endeavour of which there was much in the second half of the game. Viera had become his willing lieutenant. With Thierry Henry, not looking the full item in this company in my opinion, one still had the idea that Zidane might release him with an incisive pass and that is all Henry needs. However, he never really got a clear chance to pull the trigger. Ribéry also looked dangerous for the French as he had done throughout the tournament.

All four of these players, though, were not on the field when the extra time was completed, and so were unavailable for the shootout. Viera for the pulled hammie; Henry and Ribéry both substituted as Domenech, to his credit, tried to push a little harder, to win it the proper way – not on penalties. Zidane was not injured or substituted but indisposed for other reasons.

Zidane brought a stupendous save from Buffon in the first period of extra time.

(OR HOW I SPENT MY LONG SERVICE LEAVE)

Willy Sagnol's delightfully weighted cross, for once eluding the Italian defence, was met by the head of Zidane, who, with a hitchkick of his legs and a twist of the hips, guided the ball goalwards. You could say the contact was too good and, breathtaking though Buffon's save was, the ball was too central. More of a glance and the ball would have sliced to Buffon's right and, I fancy, left him groping thin air.

After the penalty kick artistry, Zidane's triumph then would possibly have been complete. However, less than ten minutes later he was to leave the arena in ignominy. We may never know the full story, but it appears there had been running banter between Zidane and Materazzi (and maybe other Italian defenders) throughout the game. Behind the action, for we only saw it in replay, there was what seemed to be a verbal altercation between the two players.

Zidane trotted away and then turned on his heel, stepped towards Materazzi and head-butted him squarely in the centre of the chest in the sternum. The Italian went down in a heap and stayed down and looked as if he had been subjected to open heart surgery. We would have been disappointed in him if his fall to the ground had suggested anything less.

All three officials missed the incident and it was the intervention of Mr Cantelejo, which he is entitled to do, that pointed out Zidane's behaviour to the referee. Red card, and Zidane trudged off to the dressing room. As he left the field he had to pass, standing resplendent on a low table, the gold trophy which would be awarded to the winners.

A trophy, which he himself held aloft eight years earlier as he led France to victory in Paris. I am not sure he even noticed it, as he seemed consumed with anger at what had provoked him to such a disgraceful act. Possibly, also anger at himself as the first touches of realisation kicked in.

The following day there were suggestions that Cantalejo had actually used a pitch-side monitor to see the incident in replay, and only then informed the referee's assistant who relayed the information to the referee. This is not allowed.

The officials could only then act during the game on the basis of what they see on the field of play. FIFA quickly closed ranks and denied he had used the video replay.

Final

9 July 2006, Olympic Stadium, Berlin

| **Italy** | 1 : 1 | **France** |

(aet)

| Materazzi 19' | | Zidane 7' (pen) |

Penalty shootout: Italy won 5-3:

Pirlo (scored)	Wiltord (scored)
Materazzi (scored)	Trezeguet (missed)
De Rossi (scored)	Abidal (scored)
Del Piero (scored)	Sagnol (scored)
Grosso (scored)	

Referee: Horacio Elizondo (Argentina)

Attendance: 69,000

(OR HOW I SPENT MY LONG SERVICE LEAVE)

There is no joy in being able to say that you went out to the eventual winners. However, as a piece of totally spurious research, I checked the Italian press to see if there was a journalist who might have the self-consciousness to pause for thought and ponder on Italy's luck in progressing past Australia in the Round of 16. The killjoy, if you like, that you would be bound to find somewhere in a corner of our newspapers and perhaps those in the UK, I reckon.

The day after the final, and the day after that, I went to the website of Italy's famous sports newspaper, *Gazzetta dello Sport*, and used the search facility to find any references to the word 'Australia.' *Articoli Trovati* (Articles Found or Results)? It was a round number. In fact, it was a very round number – zero!!

Typing in Lucas Neill identified just one article which appeared in May. Yet it was late June when Lucas Neill upended Grosso - according to Mr Cantalejo.

The Italians had rewritten history. Australia, the Socceroos, Lucas Neill, Italy coming so close to being out of the World Cup in Kaiserslautern, 26th June 2006, never happened.

APPENDIX
RESULTS AND FINAL STANDINGS

Group A

DATE	VENUE	TEAMS	RESULTS
9 June	Munich	Germany vs Costa Rica	4 : 2
9 June	Gelsenkirchen	Poland vs Ecuador	0 : 2
14 June	Dortmund	Germany vs Poland	1 : 0
15 June	Hamburg	Ecuador vs Costa Rica	3 : 0
20 June	Berlin	Ecuador vs Germany	0 : 3
20 June	Hanover	Costa Rica vs Poland	1 : 2

Final table

	COUNTRY	P	W	D	L	GF	GA	Pts
1	Germany	3	3	0	0	8	2	9
2	Ecuador	3	2	0	1	5	3	6
3	Poland	3	1	0	2	2	4	3
4	Costa Rica	3	0	0	3	3	9	0

RESULTS AND FINAL STANDINGS

Group B

DATE	VENUE	TEAMS	RESULTS
10 June	Frankfurt	England vs Paraguay	1 : 0
10 June	Dortmund	Trinidad & Tobago vs Sweden	0 : 0
15 June	Nuremberg	England vs Trinidad & Tobago	2 : 0
15 June	Berlin	Sweden vs Paraguay	1 : 0
20 June	Cologne	Sweden vs England	2 : 2
20 June	Kaiserslautern	Paraguay vs Trinidad & Tobago	2 : 0

Final table

	COUNTRY	P	W	D	L	GF	GA	Pts
1	England	3	2	1	0	5	2	7
2	Sweden	3	1	2	0	3	2	5
3	Paraguay	3	1	0	2	2	2	3
4	Trinidad & Tobago	3	0	1	2	0	4	1

APPENDIX

Group C

DATE	VENUE	TEAMS	RESULTS
10 June	Hamburg	Argentina vs Côte d'Ivoire	2 : 1
11 June	Leipzig	Serbia & Montenegro vs Netherlands	0 : 1
16 June	Gelsenkirchen	Argentina vs Serbia & Montenegro	6 : 0
16 June	Stuttgart	Netherlands vs Côte d'Ivoire	2 : 1
21 June	Frankfurt	Netherlands vs Argentina	0 : 0
21 June	Munich	Côte d'Ivoire vs Serbia & Montenegro	3 : 2

Final table

	COUNTRY	P	W	D	L	GF	GA	Pts
1	Argentina	3	2	1	0	8	1	7
2	Netherlands	3	2	1	0	3	1	7
3	Côte d'Ivoire	3	1	0	2	5	6	3
4	Serbia & Montenegro	3	0	0	3	2	10	0

RESULTS AND FINAL STANDINGS

Group D

DATE	VENUE	TEAMS	RESULTS
11 June	Nuremberg	Mexico vs Iran	3 : 1
11 June	Cologne	Angola vs Portugal	0 : 1
16 June	Hanover	Mexico vs Angola	0 : 0
17 June	Frankfurt	Portugal vs Iran	2 : 0
21 June	Gelsenkirchen	Portugal vs Mexico	2 : 1
21 June	Leipzig	Iran vs Angola	1 : 1

Final table

	COUNTRY	P	W	D	L	GF	GA	Pts
1	Portugal	3	3	0	0	5	1	9
2	Mexico	3	1	1	1	4	3	4
3	Angola	3	0	2	1	1	2	2
4	Iran	3	0	1	2	2	6	1

APPENDIX

Group E

DATE	VENUE	TEAMS	RESULTS
12 June	Gelsenkirchen	USA vs Czech Republic	0 : 3
12 June	Hanover	Italy vs Ghana	2 : 0
17 June	Cologne	Czech Republic vs Ghana	0 : 2
17 June	Kaiserslautern	Italy vs USA	1 : 1
22 June	Hamburg	Czech Republic vs Italy	0 : 2
22 June	Nuremberg	Ghana vs USA	2 : 1

Final table

	COUNTRY	P	W	D	L	GF	GA	Pts
1	Italy	3	2	1	0	5	1	7
2	Ghana	3	2	0	1	4	3	6
3	Czech Republic	3	1	0	2	3	4	3
4	USA	3	0	1	2	2	6	1

RESULTS AND FINAL STANDINGS

Group F

DATE	VENUE	TEAMS	RESULTS
12 June	Kaiserslautern	Australia vs Japan	3 : 1
13 June	Berlin	Brazil vs Croatia	1 : 0
18 June	Nuremberg	Japan vs Croatia	0 : 0
18 June	Munich	Brazil vs Australia	2 : 0
22 June	Dortmund	Japan vs Brazil	1 : 4
22 June	Stuttgart	Croatia vs Australia	2 : 2

Final table

	COUNTRY	P	W	D	L	GF	GA	Pts
1	Brazil	3	3	0	0	7	1	9
2	Australia	3	1	1	1	5	5	4
3	Croatia	3	0	2	1	2	3	2
4	Japan	3	0	1	2	2	7	1

APPENDIX

Group G

DATE	VENUE	TEAMS	RESULTS
13 June	Frankfurt	Korea Republic vs Togo	2 : 1
13 June	Stuttgart	France vs Switzerland	0 : 0
18 June	Leipzig	France vs Korea Republic	1 : 1
19 June	Dortmund	Togo vs Switzerland	0 : 2
23 June	Cologne	Togo vs France	0 : 2
23 June	Hanover	Switzerland vs Korea Republic	2 : 0

Final table

	COUNTRY	P	W	D	L	GF	GA	Pts
1	Switzerland	3	2	1	0	4	0	7
2	France	3	1	2	0	3	1	5
3	Korea Republic	3	1	1	1	3	4	4
4	Togo	3	0	0	3	1	6	0

RESULTS AND FINAL STANDINGS

Group H

DATE	VENUE	TEAMS	RESULTS
14 June	Leipzig	Spain vs Ukraine	4 : 0
14 June	Munich	Tunisia vs Saudi Arabia	2 : 2
19 June	Hamburg	Saudi Arabia vs Ukraine	0 : 4
19 June	Stuttgart	Spain vs Tunisia	3 : 1
23 June	Kaiserslautern	Saudi Arabia vs Spain	0 : 1
23 June	Berlin	Ukraine vs Tunisia	1 : 0

Final table

	COUNTRY	P	W	D	L	GF	GA	Pts
1	Spain	3	3	0	0	8	1	9
2	Ukraine	3	2	0	1	5	4	6
3	Saudi Arabia	3	0	1	2	2	7	1
4	Tunisia	3	0	1	2	3	6	1

APPENDIX

Round of 16

DATE	VENUE	TEAMS	RESULTS
24 June	Munich	Germany vs Sweden	2 : 0
24 June	Leipzig	Argentina vs Mexico	2 : 1
		Argentina won (aet)	
25 June	Stuttgart	England vs Ecuador	1 : 0
25 June	Nuremberg	Portugal vs Netherlands	1 : 0
26 June	Kaiserslautern	Italy vs Australia	1 : 0
26 June	Cologne	Switzerland vs Ukraine	0 : 0
		Ukraine won on penalties 0 : 3 (aet)	
27 June	Dortmund	Brazil vs Ghana	3 : 0
27 June	Hanover	Spain vs France	1 : 3

RESULTS AND FINAL STANDINGS

Quarter-Finals

DATE	VENUE	TEAMS	RESULTS
30 June	Berlin	Germany vs Argentina	1 : 1
		Germany won on penalties 4 : 2 (aet)	
30 June	Hamburg	Italy vs Ukraine	3 : 0
1 July	Gelsenkirchen	England vs Portugal	0 : 0
		Portugal won on penalties 1 : 3 (aet)	
1 July	Frankfurt	Brazil vs France	0 : 1

Semi-Finals

DATE	VENUE	TEAMS	RESULTS
4 July	Dortmund	Germany vs Italy	0 : 2
		Italy won (aet)	
5 July	Munich	Portugal vs France	0 : 1

APPENDIX

Third Place

DATE	VENUE	TEAMS	RESULT
8 July	Stuttgart	Germany vs Portugal	3 : 1

Final

DATE	VENUE	TEAMS	RESULT
9 July	Berlin	Italy vs France	1 : 1
		Italy won on penalties 5 : 3 (aet)	

ACKNOWLEDGEMENTS

There are six people to thank for this book. First and foremost, my dear wife Nicola, who, quite simply, didn't just allow me but, rather, encouraged me to follow my dream.

Our dear friend Ingrid with whom I stayed in Berlin. I told Ingrid as far back as 2000, that if Germany won the right to host the comp in 2006 then come what may, I was going to be there. Ingrid was generous to a fault in her hospitality. She also loaned me a bike to get to the railway station for the first stage of my many journeys around the country!!

My great friends Jim Smith and Marj Timberlake. They were the catalyst for this book which was firstly a diary. Before I left for Germany they urged me to let them know how I was going, and when I did send them reports they encouraged me all the more. The book reads, in part, like a diary (a blog as the modern vernacular would have it, I suppose) and owes much to my emails to them. Thank you, Jim and Marj, for your enthusiasm.

My sincere thanks to my editors David Jaggar and Lynne Kirkland. Thank you David for your encouragement – always. Thank you Lynne for your guidance, not to mention your forensic thoroughness.

So, if you enjoy the read, really you should thank them. If not, well, then that's my fault for not doing them justice.

More really good
football books
from
Fair Play Publishing

FAIRPLAY

PUBLISHING

Encyclopedia of Socceroos
by Andrew Howe

Encyclopedia of Matildas
by Andrew Howe and Greg Werner

The World Cup Chronicles
31 Days that Rocked Brazil
by Jorge Knijnik

Support Your Local League
A South East Asian Football Odyssey
by Antony Sutton

Introducing Jarrod Black
by Texi Smith

Jarrod Black - Hospital Pass
by Texi Smith

If I Started to Cry I Wouldn't Stop
by Matthew Hall

Surfing for England - Our Lost Socceroos
by Jason Goldsmith

The Aboriginal Soccer Tribe
by John Maynard

Chronicles of Soccer in Australia
The Foundation Years 1859 to 1949
by Peter Kunz

Playing for Australia
The First Socceroos, Asia and World Football
by Trevor Thompson

From US partners, Powderhouse Press:

Whatever It Takes
The Inside Story of the FIFA Way
by Bonita Mersiades

Find them all at
www.fairplaypublishing.com.au

www.ingramcontent.com/pod-product-compliance
Lightning Source LLC
Chambersburg PA
CBHW081230080526
44587CB00022B/3880